Praise for *School of the Spirit*

I grew up in a church where I never once heard the Holy Spirit mentioned. I was born again for years before anyone taught me about the third Person of the Godhead. The Holy Spirit transformed my life and my family. This book by my dear friend Lee M. Cummings is a treasure of practical knowledge that will take you to another level in your relationship with the Holy Spirit and your ability to live a life of fullness and victory!

Jimmy Evans
Best-Selling Author
Founder of MarriageToday

The Holy Spirit has promised to teach, strengthen, help, guide, fill, convict, and answer you. He'll tell you things to come, and He'll pray for you. This book is a guide to accessing this sweet relationship with the Holy Spirit. In this easy read, Pastor Lee skillfully helps us open more and more to the Holy Spirit's wonderful role in our lives.

Bob Sorge
Author of *Secrets of the Secret Place*

We live in a time of history where it has become clear that the Church cannot thrive while coasting along traditional denominational and theological lines or relying on historic Christian influence. We need the power of God to fill us and awaken us for His mission in this increasingly secular age. In this biblically accurate and stirring book, Lee paints a picture of how the Holy Spirit can both fill and empower us again to bear the fruit of God's kingdom in these important times. You will be equipped and inspired for a fresh encounter with the Holy Spirit in your life.

Jon Tyson
Lead Pastor of Church of the City New York
Author of *Beautiful Resistance*

Lee Cummings is a remarkable mixture of intelligence and anointing, a rare combination in the Western Church today. That unique mix is evident in his book *School of the Spirit*. From the first chapter where he documents why the Western Church lacks the supernatural to the last chapter where he intelligently explains the infilling of the Holy Spirit, this book goes point by point over the inward work and empowering work of the Holy Spirit that is available to each of us. I've read a lot of books about the Holy Spirit and have written a few myself, but *School of the Spirit* goes right to the top of my list of favorites. This book should be required reading for anyone who wants to go further in their walk with the Lord.

Rick Renner
Moscow, Russia
Author, Broadcaster, Pastor, Teacher

In *School of the Spirit* Lee Cummings practically teaches us how to join the Word of God and the Spirit of God together so we can live Spirit-led and Spirit-empowered lives. If we are going to see the greatest revival in history since the Day of Pentecost, we must get back to the Word and Spirit. This book helps believers do just that.

Dr. R. T. Kendall
Author of *Sensitivity of the Spirit, Total Forgiveness,*
and *We've Never Been This Way Before*

How often would you drive 20 minutes with someone in your car and not say a word to them? How often have we done this to the Holy Spirit? We can boast about being Spirit-filled, but unless we become acquainted with Him and create an atmosphere in which He is welcome, there will be no filling! Understanding *the Person of the Spirit* is paramount to experiencing *the power of the Spirit*. We can do nothing of eternal worth without His empowering presence. That's why I'm thrilled that my friend Pastor Lee Cummings has written *School of the Spirit*. He is a man I respect, and I believe the truth contained within these pages will whet your appetite to know and experience God's Spirit in a new and profound way. Don't settle for the crumbs of hearsay when you can taste and see Him for yourself!

John Bevere
Minister and Best-selling Author
Co-founder of Messenger International

It has been my privilege to minister alongside Pastor Lee Cummings in a variety of settings, and it has been an honor to become a friend to this gifted man of the Spirit who lives an honest example of non-religious Christianity. I have observed that the Word and the Spirit flow together in equal measure in Lee. His passion for the Scriptures and keen revelation of the Holy Spirit have enabled Lee to write one of the best books I have read to date on living a Spirit-driven life. *School of the Spirit* is an apt title. Lee challenges the reader to see that there are always new things to learn from the Scriptures and new adventures to discover about growing in the ways of the Holy Spirit. Accessible, understandable, and inspirational are words I would use to describe this timely book that is sure to become a resource for generations to come.

E. Wayne Drain
Founding Pastor of City Church,
President of Wayne Drain Ministries
Co-author of *He Still Speaks*

Every believer needs the power, presence, and purpose the Holy Spirit brings to our relationship with Christ. In *School of the Spirit*, Pastor Lee Cummings gives biblical foundations and practical guidance for every person seeking deeper intimacy and clear direction in their service to Christ. This book is a must read in the discipleship journey!

Tom Lane
Apostolic Senior Pastor of Gateway Church
Author of *Tested and Approved*, Co-author of *He Still Speaks*

LEE M. CUMMINGS

FOREWORD BY ROBERT MORRIS

SCHOOL of the SPIRIT

Living the Holy Spirit-Empowered Life

WITH STUDY GUIDE

School of the Spirit: Living the Holy Spirit-Empowered Life

ISBN: 978-1-951227-67-8 Hardcover
ISBN: 978-1-951227-65-4 Paperback
ISBN: 978-1-951227-66-1 eBook
ISBN: 978-1-64689-302-7 Audiobook

We hope you hear from the Holy Spirit and receive God's richest blessings from this book by Gateway Press. We want to provide the highest quality resources that take the messages, music, and media of Gateway Church to the world. For more information on other resources from Gateway Publishing®, go to gatewaypublishing.com.

We gratefully acknowledge the participation of Radiant Church in this book. For more information, visit www.radiant.church.

Gateway Press, an imprint of Gateway Publishing
700 Blessed Way
Southlake, TX 76092
gatewaypublishing.com

Printed in the United States of America

21 22 23 24 25—5 4 3 2 1

DEDICATION

THIS BOOK IS DEDICATED to Pastor Wayne Benson, my role model as a young Christian. He showed me the importance of a deep dedication to the Word of God and what the Holy Spirit's power and presence can look like in a church.

TABLE OF CONTENTS

FOREWORD

WHEN MY WIFE, Debbie, and I were first married 40 years ago, our circumstances were different than they are now. I was a land surveyor with my dad's company, and we lived in a mobile home. One day we went over to a friend's house, and Debbie noticed they had a beautiful, thick comforter on their bed. Our own bedspread, a hand-me-down, was pretty old and worn out, so this one caught her attention. Later that night, Debbie told me she really wanted to buy a comforter like the one our friends had.

Soon after, I came home from work to find a beautiful, thick comforter on our bed. It was luxurious! Debbie showed me how great it looked, and then we went into the other room to eat dinner and watch TV. When we decided to go to bed a few hours later, our new comforter was gone! Someone had stolen it and put our old bedspread back on our bed!

"What happened to our new comforter?" I asked Debbie.

"Robert, that comforter is *not* for use. It's for looks!" she replied matter-of-factly.

I looked over at the end of our bed and saw that Debbie had carefully folded up our new comforter and put it away for the night. That's when I learned there are certain things in our house that are just for display—put out to look nice—but never really used for anything other than decoration. Then there are other things that are actually used for their intended purpose, such as a blanket that provides warmth. Those are real comforters. The type of comforter that's perfect after an especially long, hard day when you're physically and emotionally exhausted.

What many people don't realize is that Jesus said the Holy Spirit is our comforter. We mistakenly think He is just for looks or show, and we don't allow Him to truly comfort us when we're exhausted or going through the storms of life.

How many of us treat the Holy Spirit just like a bed comforter? We embrace the Spirit of God on the surface of our lives, but when it comes to our day-in and day-out existence, we set Him aside and use the old bedspread of our human wills and emotions. We read about what the Holy Spirit did in the Bible but miss out on the power and blessing of walking with Him on a daily basis.

The Holy Spirit wants to be your comforter, your helper, and your friend. Jesus presented the Holy Spirit to you and me so we could walk in the truth, freedom, and fullness of life He promised us in His Word. The Holy Spirit is the ultimate answer to overcoming Satan, the deceiver and "father of lies" (John 8:44). However, I've noticed a hesitancy in believers when it comes to embracing Jesus' gift of the Holy Spirit.

It shouldn't come as a surprise that the devil has done his best to make living the Holy Spirit-empowered life controversial. Think about it: If the Holy Spirit is essential for believers to live as God intended (and He is!), then doesn't it make sense that the enemy would want to keep us from experiencing all He has to offer? The devil will use whatever means necessary to get us to believe the lie that the Holy Spirit isn't for believers today. He'll say the Holy Spirit is weird, and he'll deceive people into doing bizarre things, only to claim the Holy Spirit made them do it. As a result, some people might be completely opposed to the Holy Spirit or think, *This Holy Spirit stuff is probably good but only in small doses. You just don't want to get too carried away with it.*

In essence, we tell the Holy Spirit, "Okay, I'll open the door of my life a few inches so You can stick Your foot in, but I'm not letting You come all the way in because there's no telling what You'll do. I don't trust You to behave Yourself."

The truth is, the Holy Spirit isn't weird. He's God! The Father, Son, and Holy Spirit are one God in three Persons. That's right— the Holy Spirit is a Person, and He is present and necessary to help you live the successful Christian life. He is there to give comfort, help, and friendship. He is an amazing, kind, compassionate, wonderful, and sensitive Person who knows you even better than you know yourself.

Many Christians experience defeat and disappointment because they try to live life in their own strength. They don't understand that the Holy Spirit is the One who makes victorious living possible.

If you want to know the Holy Spirit like this, you've come to the right place. My friend Lee Cummings helps you understand how to live a life fully empowered and strengthened by the friendship and intimacy that can be found only with the Holy Spirit. As the founding and senior pastor of Radiant Church, Lee has been teaching people how to operate in the gifts of the Holy Spirit at a deeper level and how to build a strong biblical foundation for Spirit-led living. After almost 25 years of teaching this message, he wrote this book to equip and train even more people to walk in the presence and gifts of the Holy Spirit. In it, you'll learn what it means to live the Holy Spirit-empowered life by discovering who the Holy Spirit is, how He acts, and what kind of a relationship you were created to have with Him.

This journey you're about to embark on may be new to you, or it might be like returning to a familiar friend. No matter where you are, though, my prayer is that you will open your heart and mind as you begin to see the Holy Spirit for who He really is. I pray you will gain a deeper understanding of what it means to experience His presence and power in your life. The Holy Spirit desires to have a relationship with you, and I know that walking in relationship with Him and experiencing the life-giving power He offers will change your life forever. It's my hope that as you read this book, you'll come to know Him in a whole new way and understand how victorious the Christian life can be with the Holy Spirit.

Robert Morris
Senior Pastor of Gateway Church
Bestselling Author of *The Blessed Life, Beyond Blessed, The God I Never Knew,* and *Take the Day Off*

ACKNOWLEDGMENTS

MOST OF THE TIME, the author of a book like this receives the credit for its content and completion, but the reality is that there are more people behind the scenes required to bring the idea into reality. *School of the Spirit* is no exception. So much of the content of this book is drawn from years of sitting under amazing and anointed teachers of the Word, such as Rick Renner, Jimmy Evans, John Wimber, and others, as well as reading many books on the subject. I am deeply indebted to those who have invested in me directly or indirectly, shaping my theology and pastoral perspective on the subject of the Holy Spirit and His gifts.

I want to acknowledge the indispensable partnership of Edie Mourey. You were able to capture my voice, shape my teaching, and help form the content of this book. Your spirit of excellence and heart-felt passion for the Lord and His Word are incomparable gifts to authors like me. Thank you for reading, writing, and Marco Polo-ing me with ideas and drafts until we got it right.

To the team at Gateway Publishing, thank you for believing in me and the message of this book. Your deep devotion to the local church and commitment to producing books and resources that honor the Spirit of God are inspiring. Thank you for partnering with me.

To my assistant for more than 10 years, Krista Kennedy, thank you for pushing me on this project and helping create the conversation with the team at Gateway Publishing. You are the best at what you do, even though I don't know all that you do (since keeping all the distracting details away from me is what you do). I'm eternally grateful.

To Rick Burmeister, my comrade in arms and Executive Pastor of Radiant Church. You, along with Krista, Cassie, Ron, and Ashley, set the stage for success and did the difficult leg work behind the scenes so that more of God's children could experience the fullness of His abiding presence and power. Heaven only knows the eternal impact your labor on this and so many other projects has made for the Kingdom of God.

Finally, there is one person who has walked with me every step of the way on this journey of ministry. It is a journey I would never and could never have taken without the support, encouragement, and inspiration of my best friend and wife, Jane. There are not enough words to express my gratitude to God for you. All I can say is thank you. I love you with my whole heart.

INTRODUCTION

WHEN I WAS about four or five years old, my grandfather often took me to do errands with him in his red Chevy truck. He called it "boondoggling." One day while we were boondoggling, my grandfather stopped at Richardson's Dairy in Clarkston, Michigan. My mother had taken me to that store before, and I really liked it because it had a huge aisle with all kinds of candy. Whenever my mom took me to Richardson's, she allowed me to pick out a penny candy (yes, I realize that was in a different century). I'd choose a small jawbreaker or sometimes a Tootsie Roll. She was a single parent, so that's all she could afford.

This time, however, my grandfather wanted to do something special for me. He said, "Lee, go pick something out. You can have *anything* you want." As usual, I headed over to the penny side of the candy aisle. I reached out to pick up a little jawbreaker, but my grandfather stopped me. He said, "No, no, no, Lee. You don't *want* that. Pick out something else."

So I scooted a little further down the aisle to the nickel candy section. I thought this was a big deal because I had just increased my vision 500 percent! I was spying out Tootsie Pops and some similar candies, but before I could make a decision, my grandfather interrupted me again. "No, no, no, no, no, Lee! That's not what you *want*. Pick out something else."

Imagine my excitement as I slid even further down the aisle to the quarter candy. I was now in uncharted territory! I saw packs of Bubblicious, a soft bubblegum. There were little paraffin wax bottle candies with flavored juice inside and Candy Dots with the pastel-colored buttons of sugar on paper. I thought, *Woo! Now we're talking!* But that still wasn't good enough for my grandfather. "No, no, no! You don't *want* that. Pick out something else, Lee."

By this point, I was confused. I looked up at him and asked, "Grandpa, what do I want?" Then he led me down to the end of the aisle, all the way to the other side, and helped me to pick out a Slo Poke Caramel Pop. To a little boy, it was humongous— big enough to row a kayak! I started drooling like a Bullmastiff, and I carried that candy pop around for a week. My grandfather was happy because he knew what I really wanted. He knew what would make me the happiest, even though I was content on the penny side of the candy aisle because that's all I knew from my previous experience.

Here's my point: We as Christians often live on the penny side of the aisle. We don't know what we really want or, more importantly, what God wants for us. Because we lack understanding and experience, we are willing to settle for humdrum, boring lives as believers. We know Jesus has saved us. We trust we will go to heaven. We attend church and even try to tell people about what Jesus can do for them. To the best of our ability, we try to live in a way that is pleasing to God, but we are missing out on the *one thing* that will make all the difference in our lives. That one thing is living in partnership with Him through the Holy Spirit.

YOUR PARTNERSHIP WITH GOD

"What do you want?" I'm sure you've heard this question before. The person asking you may have meant something as simple as what kind of candy you want from the store, but it's more serious than that. I'm not asking what kind of food you want for breakfast, what kind of car you want to drive, or even what kind of job you want. I mean this: *What do you want for your life?* When we hear that question, many of us struggle to give an answer. Like a little boy on the penny side of the candy aisle, we don't realize there's something *more* available to us— something beyond what we can imagine or dream.

You probably remember hearing this question for the first time as a child. Someone asked you what you wanted *to be* when you grew up. Your parents and teachers tried to get you to think about the direction your life would take so they could properly prepare you for the future. I heard that question over and over again as I was growing into adulthood. However, this question doesn't stop on your eighteenth birthday. The truth is, we will be answering it for the rest of our lives.

Our culture is consumer-driven. People look for the things they think will give them the most fulfillment, even though they don't know what a fulfilled life actually is. What would happen if we rejected the cultural expectations and started living according to what God wants for us as citizens of His Kingdom? The Kingdom of God isn't "me-centric." In fact, it truly has nothing to do with what we want and everything to do with what God wants. "What do you want?" Can you see how this question changes as you try to follow Jesus? It transforms into "God, what do You want? (Because I want what You want!)"

I wrote this book to help you ask God two very basic yet very important questions:

1. God, what do You want?
2. How can I hear You when You answer?

JESUS: OUR PATTERN

Throughout His earthly life, Jesus showed us how to be partners with God, as we are anointed by the Holy Spirit just as He was. Jesus is our model for how to be truly human. Other words to describe this relationship between His life and how we should live ours include *pattern, prototype,* and *exemplar* (which means "example"). Jesus came not only to deliver us from sin, death, hell, and the devil but also to establish the pattern for how we should live as human beings in cooperation with the Father and through the Holy Spirit. Jesus shows us how to live beyond ourselves. Ours is a life of faith, which recognizes the reality of God's supernatural activity in our present world. Jesus' life and ministry show us how the Holy Spirit is at work in every aspect of life—both His and ours.

> *Jesus' life and ministry show us how the Holy Spirit is at work in every aspect of life—both His and ours.*

When do we first see the Holy Spirit working in the life of Jesus? It was long before His public ministry began. In fact, it was at the very beginning of the New Testament—at Jesus' conception. The Bible opens in Genesis 1 with the Spirit brooding over the water that covered the earth. In Matthew's gospel, the Holy Spirit hovers once again, this time over the depth and waters of Mary's womb (see Luke 1:35). Nine months later, Jesus, the Word who was present at Creation and became flesh at conception, enters the world, and lives among people just like us (see John 1:14).

We see the Holy Spirit present and at work not only at Jesus' conception but also during His childhood and throughout His adult ministry. The Holy Spirit manifested at His baptism, for example. Jesus made an appearance at the Jordan River where His cousin John was baptizing people and calling them to turn away from sin ("Repent!") in preparation for the coming of the Messiah. This location was the same place where the Israelites crossed hundreds of years earlier as they passed into the Promised Land. This time, however, God didn't split the Jordan for the people to cross. Instead, He tore open the heavens, and the Holy Spirit came down. Jesus stepped into the water, John baptized Him, and the Spirit of God came down upon Jesus like a dove. At that moment, John recognized Jesus as the Messiah because the Holy Spirit was the promised sign for which he had been looking. The Holy Spirit publicly anointed Jesus, inaugurating His ministry. Then, God the Father confirmed it, saying in a voice for all to hear, "You are my beloved Son; with you I am well pleased" (Luke 3:22).

Luke's gospel says Jesus left the Jordan River "full of the Holy Spirit" (4:1), and Mark's gospel records that "the Spirit immediately drove [Jesus] out into the wilderness" (1:12). There, the devil tempted Jesus for 40 days. Then Jesus returned from the wilderness with evidence of the Holy Spirit's power in His life (Luke 4:14).

Next, Jesus attended the synagogue in His hometown of Nazareth. He unfurled the scroll of Isaiah's prophecy and began reading:

> The Spirit of the Lord is upon me,
>   because he has anointed me
>   to proclaim good news to the poor.
> He has sent me to proclaim liberty to the captives
>   and recovering of sight to the blind,
>   to set at liberty those who are oppressed,
> to proclaim the year of the Lord's favor
> (Luke 4:18–19; see also Isaiah 61:1–2).

As Jesus read, everyone in the synagogue understood that He was revealing the mission statement of His ministry. Then, setting the scroll aside, Jesus said, "Today this Scripture has been fulfilled in your hearing" (Luke 4:21). The Spirit of the Lord was in Him and upon Him to do good—to heal those who were sick and oppressed, to free those who were in prison, to give and restore sight and life. The apostle Peter confirms Jesus did all these things during His earthly life: "God anointed Jesus of Nazareth with the Holy Spirit and with power. He went about doing good and healing all who were oppressed by the devil, for God was with him" (Acts 10:38).

Jesus humbled Himself and became a human being like us (see Philippians 2:6–11). Because He is now and forever our pattern, we should also humble ourselves and become like Him. God didn't create us to live according to the way the world works but according to the pattern of Jesus. And Jesus lived in absolute dependence on the Holy Spirit and in perfect obedience to the Father.

Jesus never tried to compartmentalize portions of His life by saying, "I will follow the Holy Spirit in most matters, but in these things, I just can't do it." Jesus didn't occasionally check in with the Holy Spirit when trouble came or when it felt convenient. The Holy Spirit didn't come upon Jesus every once in a while. No, Jesus' life was intricately woven together with the Holy Spirit. Theirs was (and is) a true partnership.

Jesus gave us a model for our relationship with the Holy Spirit. He showed us how to walk in the Spirit's power and anointing. Jesus taught us how to be led by the Spirit in our work just as He was in His. Our lives as Christians will never be dull or ordinary. No more status-quo Christianity for us. No more settling for the penny side of the candy aisle. God is calling us right now to live supernatural lives. He wants us to live the adventure of *the Holy-Spirit-empowered life.*

The Holy Spirit was the One who empowered everything Jesus did, and we also should be driven and empowered by the Spirit. God calls us as His children to live naturally supernatural lives. We may sometimes have problems thinking this way because we aren't quite sure how living in and with the Spirit will translate into our everyday existence. Often, we lack the necessary frame of reference, so we are hesitant to embrace all the Spirit has for us, and we don't give Him complete control.

The Holy Spirit was the One who empowered everything Jesus did, and we also should be driven and empowered by the Spirit.

THE MOST MISUNDERSTOOD PERSON OF THE TRINITY

I was really young when I first heard about the Holy Spirit. My grandparents took me to a tiny Pentecostal church, and as a four- or five-year-old boy, all I knew was that those church services seemed *so long*. Even more challenging, everyone had to sit in wooden theater-style seats on cold, tiled floors. I knelt on those hard floors, pulled down my seat, and use it as a desk. Then I drew pictures on scraps of paper until the service mercifully came to an end.

I admit I didn't pay much attention to what was happening in the service until one day I heard a man in our congregation speak in a way I had not heard before. His name was Tuppy Mudge, and he was a large man who stood at least six-and-a-half-feet tall. I remember he kept a Gideon New Testament tucked into his jacket. Over the prayers and praise of the rest of the congregation, I heard Tuppy shout, "Whooooa!" Then he reached into his pocket and pulled out the New Testament. As he held it in his hand, he began to speak with authority and power. Though I didn't understand it at the time, Tuppy was prophesying to the church.

Tuppy's massive size and booming voice overwhelmed me. I remember feeling frightened as this giant of a man waved that New Testament and prophesied. I turned to my grandmother and asked, "What's going on?!" She must have recognized the panic in my voice. "The Holy Ghost is here," she whispered in my ear. Maybe she thought I would understand what she meant. She might have even been trying to console me. Or she wanted me to at least hush. Now you know I was in a genuine Pentecostal church because people would often refer to the Holy Spirit as "the Holy Ghost!"

I only had one image in my mind for a ghost at that time, and that was from the cartoon series *Casper the Friendly Ghost*, which I sometimes watched on Saturday mornings. That show, along with *Scooby-Doo, Where Are You!* and a handful of other movie ghosts, made up my entire understanding of that concept. I thought ghosts floated around and scared everybody. So when my grandmother told me the Holy Ghost was in our church service, I quickly hid under my seat. I was expecting it to zoom around the room, and I was terrified!

My first memory of the Holy Spirit wasn't the best representation. Still, it colored everything I knew about Him throughout my childhood and into my adolescent years. Then as a teen, I finally discovered the Holy Spirit isn't scary or weird. He doesn't haunt us. He is the Spirit of God and a distinct and equal member of the Trinity, made up of the Father, the Son, *and* the Holy Spirit. As I grew in faith, I came to know that the Holy Spirit is the closest Person of the Godhead that you and I relate to on a daily basis as followers of Jesus Christ.

As a pastor and student of the Bible, I also recognize that the Holy Spirit is the most misunderstood Person of the Godhead. When Christians speak of the Trinity, we feel comfortable talking about the Father and the Son because we can relate to human fathers and sons. We know what fathers are, whether one was present or not in our childhood. We also know about sons, because we either are a son or know sons. However, once we get to the matter of the Holy Spirit, things get a little fuzzy, and we lose traction. We don't have as clear a frame of reference for Him out of our life experiences as we do for the Father and the Son.

In John's gospel, Jesus has a conversation with a man named Nicodemus about being "born again" or "born of the Spirit" (see John 3:1–21). The theological term for this experience is *regeneration*, and it is a work that the Holy Spirit does in us. (We will discuss this more later.) Jesus says to Nicodemus, "The wind blows where it wishes, and you hear its sound, but you do not know where it comes from or where it goes. So it is with everyone who is born of the Spirit" (v. 8). According to Jesus, the new birth is a work of the Spirit. In a way, it is mysterious and ethereal. The Holy Spirit makes you brand new, yet you can't completely define the experience. You know you've been affected by Him, but you can't quite get a handle on Him or grab ahold of Him. Jesus said the Holy Spirit is much like the wind. You probably even have a difficult time trying to describe to others what He has done to you and in you. After all, you can't draw a picture of the Holy Spirit or make a visual representation of what He has done in your life. All you can do is say, "He's changed my life. I was once ... and now I'm ..."

We try to capture the Holy Spirit to study and control Him. However, I must tell you that you will never catch Him. As Jesus said, it would be like trying to harness the wind. The Spirit will not be controlled by anyone or anything. We are usually very uncomfortable with things outside of our definition or control. You may even feel like I did as a little boy in a church service who didn't have the right frame of reference. You may think of the Holy Spirit as a haunting, scary ghost. When we don't have a grid for something we're experiencing or something others tell us about, then it's easy to feel uncomfortable or to find ourselves paralyzed by fear.

We begin here. Jesus is the pattern for the Holy Spirit-empowered life, yet we still don't completely understand how living in the Spirit will play out in our everyday existence. We are left asking ourselves these questions:

- What does being led by the Spirit look like in my life?
- What does He want to do in and through me?
- How can I walk in step with Him?
- What part do I play in this partnership?
- Does this mean I'll have to receive the baptism of the Holy Spirit?
- Will I have to speak in tongues?

I want to help you answer these crucial questions in *School of the Spirit*. Not only do I want to help you discover more about the Holy Spirit in you, but I also want to show you how to live the Spirit-empowered life. Throughout this book, I will show you what the Bible says about the Holy Spirit and how our culture has a distorted view of Him. I will reveal what Jesus said about the Holy Spirit, discuss the Father's promise, and lay out the benefits of the baptism and gifts of Spirit. In this book, you'll discover what the Holy Spirit does in us and what it will be like to walk daily in His power.

I have organized this book in the style of a college course. Each section has a course number like you would see in a college catalog (e.g., 101, 201, and 301). I follow a planned progression in each subsequent section to help you learn about the Holy Spirit so you can develop in your partnership with Him. Nevertheless, you'll notice there isn't a section named School of the Spirit 401. Why? Because there's no graduation from this school until you get to heaven. When you finish *School of the Spirit*, my greatest desire is for you to keep growing and developing your partnership with the Spirit throughout your life. This is just the beginning.

> When the Spirit of truth comes, he will guide you into all the truth, for he will not speak on his own authority, but whatever he hears he will speak, and he will declare to you the things that are to come. He will glorify me, for he will take what is mine and declare it to you (John 16:13–14).

It wouldn't be right to begin this study by leaving the Holy Spirit out of it. We can't say, "Thanks, Holy Spirit. We've got it from here." No, we need His help. So before moving into the first chapter, join me in asking the Holy Spirit to teach us, lead us, and guide us into the truth.

> *Holy Spirit, we ask You, according to Ephesians 1, to release upon us a spirit of wisdom, revelation, and enlightenment as we begin this journey. God, open our hearts to see the hope of our calling, to*

know the inheritance we have in the saints, and to understand the depth of Your power at work in our lives. Holy Spirit, we ask You to come. Come and open our eyes. Come and illuminate the truth of Your Word as You prepare our hearts to receive it. Lead us into an encounter with You that forever changes us and deepens our love for Jesus. That's our prayer. In Jesus' name, Amen.

SCHOOL OF THE SPIRIT 101

INTRODUCTION
TO THE HOLY SPIRIT

CHAPTER 1

MAKING THE CONNECTION

For people will be lovers of self, lovers of money, proud, arrogant, abusive, disobedient to their parents, ungrateful, unholy, heartless, unappeasable, slanderous, without self-control, brutal, not loving good, treacherous, reckless, swollen with conceit, lovers of pleasure rather than lovers of God, having the appearance of godliness, but denying its power. Avoid such people.

—The apostle Paul in 2 Timothy 3:2–5

LET'S PLAY A word association game. I say a word or phrase, and you respond with the first thing that comes to your mind. Are you ready? Okay, here we go. "Holy Spirit." What just came to your mind? Did you think of *power, freedom, comfort, help, guide,* or *God?* If so, why did any of those words come to mind?

We must begin our journey with a foundational truth: the Holy Spirit is first and foremost God Himself. Contrary to what many people think, the Holy Spirit is not an impersonal force or an energy field. He is a Person with a capital "P." The Holy Spirit isn't merely a personality such as an angel or some other kind of spirit. No, He is fully and completely God. He is divine and the third member of the Trinity.

> *The Holy Spirit is first and foremost God Himself.*

3

HOW DID WE GET TO THIS POINT?

In the first few centuries of the Church, Christian leaders gathered in official councils to help the Church define true teaching (orthodoxy) and separate it from false teaching (heresy). They saw the danger of false teaching infecting the Church, and they wanted to stop it. One of the major questions they addressed had to with the nature of God, including how the Church was to understand and define the Holy Spirit. These Church leaders determined that the nature of the Trinity (also called the "Godhead") is as follows: God is one God, all three members of the Trinity eternally co-exist, and each member of the Trinity is a distinct Person who dwells together in unity with the other two. When you hear the word "Trinity," it will help you to think of it as a "tri-unity." These early church leaders described the Holy Spirit as

The Lord, the giver of life,
who proceeds from the Father [and the Son],
who with the Father and the Son is adored and glorified.[1]

Accordingly, the Holy Spirit is not merely the projection of God's will. Neither is He the energy proceeding from God to accomplish God's purposes. No, the early church councils concluded that the Holy Spirit was and is, in fact, God Himself.

Today, the Church consists of many denominations, traditions, and expressions, all of which emerged since the Nicene Creed was first crafted by those early Church leaders. All these different churches (with a lowercase "c") seem to have more to say about their particular way of administering water baptism than they do about how we are to understand and relate to the Person of the Holy Spirit. In reality, however, Jesus taught much more about the Holy Spirit than water baptism. I do not say this because I think water baptism is unimportant, but because the relationship we have as believers with the Holy Spirit is vital for an effective Christian life.

Christians have often treated the Holy Spirit as if He were an add-on appendage to their basic salvation or a silent partner in their lives. But as I look at the life and ministry of Jesus and study the early church, I recognize that the Holy Spirit is in no way silent. He is very present and very vocal. Water baptism is a one-time event, an initiation into a life of following Jesus with reckless abandon, but the Holy Spirit is our *ever-present* Helper, Guide, and Teacher. He leads us on this lifelong journey. If we know the Holy Spirit personally and pursue His leadership, then He will teach us the things we need to know for success along our journey. We shouldn't minimize Jesus' teaching about the Holy Spirit and turn it into something optional, nor should we think about it as a doctrinal distinctive that belongs only to certain kinds of Christians. Jesus taught that the Holy Spirit is alive and available to *all* believers. Speaking about the promised Spirit, the apostle Peter said, "The promise is for you and for your children and for all who are far off, everyone whom the Lord our God calls to himself" (Acts 2:39).

Jesus taught that the Holy Spirit is alive and available to all believers.

One of the sad truths regarding Western Christianity is that the older historical denominations have inherited a rich doctrinal tradition through the great creeds of the Church, yet something vital is missing. These valuable creeds give useful words and formulas to help us define our faith. Even so, the historical bastions of strength for these denominations in Western Europe and North America are rapidly shrinking. As of today, no full-blown revival or spiritual awakening is on the horizon. But we are witnessing a resurgence of interest in the Holy Spirit. Perhaps His work in the lives of these Christians is a smoldering ember, awaiting a fresh fanning that will explode into a raging inferno of the Holy Spirit's power and presence.

Nevertheless, we do not worship a sleepy God, and the Holy Spirit is not taking a nap. Right now, a mighty move of the Holy Spirit has fallen on Africa, Asia, and Latin America. In those regions, there are approximately 1.6 billion Christians[2] (more than half of the 2.5 billion Christians in the world today[3]). Almost 600 million Christians identify as Charismatic or Pentecostal[4], and they are igniting the world with the Good News of Jesus under the Spirit's manifest power. Most of these believers live below the Equator and in the Eastern Hemisphere. The Holy Spirit is on the move globally in an unprecedented way. You may not see it or know it, but His action is real and evident. In many places, the Holy Spirit is moving in power, signs, and wonders that now eclipse anything we read about in the book of Acts. The gospel *is* going forward!

Even in the Middle East, a region that has historically resisted the gospel, the Holy Spirit has pinpointed a special place for His movement in our present day. According to *The Christian Post*, "researchers have credited the underground church in

Iran as the fastest-growing Christian church in the world."[5] In 1979 there were only 500 Christians in Iran, but in 2017, there were 360,000.[6] It's as if God is saying, "I'm just going to show up and show off in this region and among these people where I've been told I can't. Indeed, I can. And I am going to do it right now!"

So why isn't the Western Church experiencing the same revival intensity? I believe it is because of our culture's bias against the supernatural.[7] Many Christians have excluded the activity and presence of the Holy Spirit from their individual and corporate lives. The disconnect originated with the secular sources that enveloped the western world during the Renaissance and Enlightenment periods but then were adopted by many western Christians as early as the Protestant Reformation. This philosophical and theological shift became known as *modernism*.

THE WESTERN BIAS AGAINST THE SUPERNATURAL

To understand what happened to the Church as a result of modernism, we will first have to discuss its place historically. During the Renaissance (ca. 1400–1600), classical Greco-Roman art, literature, and philosophy were rediscovered or reemphasized. Prior to the Renaissance, the Roman Catholic Church, supernaturalism, and superstition held the most cultural sway in the west. Western explorers and missionaries began to move into previously unknown lands and encounter new people groups. Scientific discoveries began to unlock and explain a world that had previously been hidden from western understanding. Amid this knowledge explosion came the invention of the printing press with moveable type, which quickly disseminated the newly discovered information and led to a human-centric understanding of the universe.

The Renaissance helped to birth the Enlightenment era (c. 1700s), in which the empirical and scientific methods, logic, and reason took precedence. Historians often refer to the Enlightenment as the *Age of Reason*. Human reasoning, individualism, and skepticism reigned during this period. Even in philosophy and theology, truth and belief became subject to the scientific method. Christianity had formed and shaped European society and Western civilization, but Enlightenment philosophy emerged as a formidable challenger. It ushered in a new form of humanism and a human-centered approach to the world. With its emphasis on science and reason, the Enlightenment then gave birth to modernism.

Modernism, as a movement, arrived in the late nineteenth century. Modernist philosophers and theologians sought to modify traditional beliefs with new, modern ideas. Modernists reacted against traditional religious, political, and social views and rejected the notion of absolute truth. For example, modernist theologians began to challenge the authority of Scripture, the historicity of Jesus, and the miracles of the virgin birth and the Resurrection. They attempted to apply the empirical method[8] anachronistically to the Bible, central Christian doctrines, and miraculous events. Modernism embraced an empirical and materialistic worldview. If something could not be touched and measured, then it could not exist. Consequently, the unseen God, the soul, miracles, and

8

the supernatural became subject to skepticism and outright denial.

Modernist philosophy seeped into every aspect of life and continues to influence us today. Trying to explain to a fellow person the ways he or she has been influenced by modernism is like trying to tell a fish what life is like in water. It has bled into our educational system, businesses, industries, politics, and government. Tragically, it also has affected how we understand Christianity, engage with God's Word, and relate to the Holy Spirit.

HOW THE WESTERN CHURCH EXCLUDED THE HOLY SPIRIT'S ACTIVITY

While secular forces were setting the scene for modernism within Western culture, Martin Luther was seeking the Lord and the truth in the early 1500s. In his quest to establish a right relationship with God, this Catholic monk tried to do everything possible within the confines of the Roman Catholic Church. Luther fasted and even flogged himself in an effort to prove a heart of true repentance and devotion to God. Then, one day, while reading and studying the apostle Paul's Letter to the Romans, Luther had a life-changing encounter with God. He realized that God's grace was the only way for us to have faith and, concurrently, that faith was the only way for us to be justified before God. This bombshell of a revelation transformed the Western Church and still is transforming it today. Luther soon began to publicly address some of the more egregious abuses he had witnessed within the Catholic

Church. On October 31, 1517, Luther nailed a list of disputes to the door of the Wittenberg Cathedral. Known today as the *Ninety-five Theses* (or *Disputation on the Power and Efficacy of Indulgences*), this document set into motion the Protestant Reformation and forever divided the Western Church.

Luther and other Reformation leaders stood against many of the excesses and superstitions that had crept into the Catholic Church. These reformers opposed practices such as the veneration of saints' bones, the selling of indulgences[9], and other unbiblical rituals and traditions the Catholic Church was putting forward as means for people to receive God's grace and favor. Reacting to these excesses, Luther declared *three solas*; *sola scriptura* ('by Scripture alone'), *sola fide* ('by faith alone'), and *sola gratia* ('by grace alone')—and all of these to the glory of God alone.

Luther and the other reformers encouraged the Church to stick to the Bible, faith, and grace. As a movement, then, the Reformation focused on the cross of Christ, led people into salvation, and then encouraged them to grow in faith. These reformers proclaimed that reading and learning from the Bible was the best way for believers to gain wisdom and theological understanding. To that end, Luther personally took on the task of translating the Bible into German, the mother tongue of his people.[10] Before this time, only scholars and theologians could read the Bible. Even most local priests could not read it; they were insufficiently trained to read Latin, let alone Greek, Hebrew, or Aramaic.

Luther's desire was to make the truth of the Bible accessible to everyone in a language they could understand. In fact, William

Tyndale, an English reformer inspired by Luther, said there would come a day when a boy driving a plow would know more about the Bible than a priest.[11] Throughout Europe, Christian reformers joined in the enterprise of translating the Bible into the mother tongues of their peoples, all based on the foundational conviction that *if we have the Bible, then it is enough.*

Every great reform in the history of the Christian Church has been an attempt to correct a wrong. However, these reforms have usually been accompanied by overemphasis and overcorrections. Scripture is—and should always be—the foundational standard for our faith, but not to the exclusion of hearing God when He speaks in other ways. Instead of declaring *sola scriptura,* I would encourage believers to think of *prima scriptura,* which means Scripture is our first foundation for understanding God's voice but not the only way He communicates with us.

> *Scripture is our first foundation for understanding God's voice but not the only way He communicates with us.*

God's voice will never contradict what He has already said in the Bible. The written Word is the solid foundation for true doctrine and serves as our plumbline for pursuing and following Jesus. The Scriptures should draw us into a deeper encounter and personal relationship with the living God. Reading the Bible should provoke us into drawing closer to the Lord so we can relate to Him in many of the same ways that the people of the Bible did. Do not read and study the Bible as a means to offer God mere intellectual assent nor to gain more academic information. Knowledge alone will puff us up with pride, ultimately leaving us spiritually dissatisfied. Rather, studying the Bible should help us to hear the Holy Spirit more clearly. Information that doesn't bring about transformation is only useful if you're playing a game of Bible trivia. True transformation will develop a deep hunger within you to encounter the living God through the Person of the Holy Spirit.

God is not sitting far away in the unreachable heavens, saying, "I gave you a Book, so read it, and I'll get back with you in a couple millennia to talk more about it." No, He is saying, "I have provided this Book because I want to reveal Myself to you. I want to walk with you and make you aware of My Spirit I have put within you. I want to awaken you to the power available through Him so you can be an effective witness to the world."

For several centuries, the three *solas* have shaped Western Christianity to the exclusion of the supernatural. As a result, the Western Church developed religious traditions that extinguished the expectancy that God is present, available, and working in our world. We have missed an intimate relationship with God, lost access to His power, and turned away from following His divine leadership. We have essentially tried to practice our faith while being disconnected from its source. Consequently, American Christianity has become an amalgamation of shallow self-help, fortune cookie optimism, and occasional solid theology.

I declare that it is past time for the Western Church to embrace the supernatural, wonder-working God of the Bible. As you read this book, I pray for God to impart and restore wonder in your life. It's time for us to make the connection. We need a meaningful relationship with the living God through the Holy Spirit, the most "present" Person of the Trinity. The Spirit is the imminent, "right here" presence of God in us, personally making Him known to us. We need Him today.

Jesus, You became a human like us to show us how we should walk in relationship with the Father in the power of the Spirit. We want to walk as You did—completely in step with the Holy Spirit. We don't want to minimize His involvement in our lives. We don't want to live with the appearance of being "spiritual" while refusing to open our hearts and lives to the wonder-working power of Your Holy Spirit.

Father, please forgive us for making decisions away from Your will and apart from the Spirit's leadership and guidance. Today, we surrender anew to You. We pray for Your Kingdom to come and Your will to be done in our lives. Equip and empower us by Your Spirit for every good work. Where You lead, we will follow. In Jesus' name, Amen.

STUDY GUIDE

THE HOLY SPIRIT is first and foremost God. He is fully divine and an equal member of the Trinity. Today, many Christians in the Western Church have a disconnect due to a cultural bias against the supernatural, but the Holy Spirit is present and available to all believers. We need His guidance to succeed on our journey through life and His power to be effective witnesses to the world.

REVIEW

1. What did the early Church councils determine about the nature of the Trinity? How did they describe the Holy Spirit?
2. In what ways did Modernism influence people's view of the supernatural?
3. What is the difference between *sola scriptura* and *primara scriptura*? How does this difference affect the way believers relate to God?

REFLECTION

1. Before reading this chapter, what was your view of the Holy Spirit's nature and position in a Christian's life? What factors shaped this view?

SCHOOL OF THE SPIRIT

2. Why do you think countries such as Iran are experiencing a mighty move of the Holy Spirit with many people coming to faith in Jesus Christ, even though there is a very real risk of persecution?
3. What kind of relationship would you like to have with the Holy Spirit? How would this relationship change your day-to-day life?

CHAPTER 2

YOUR ADVANTAGE

"But you will receive power when the Holy Spirit has come upon you, and you will be my witnesses in Jerusalem and in all Judea and Samaria, and to the end of the earth."

—Jesus in Acts 1:8

I HAVE OFTEN wondered what it would have been like to have lived in the first century and been one of the 12 disciples who followed Jesus during His earthly ministry. Not long ago, I made a trip to Israel. I had the awe-inspiring experience of standing in some of the same places the Bible says Jesus taught and performed miracles and walking on some of the same paths He traveled. I thought, *Man, this is incredible! I'm actually standing where Jesus stood.*

The experiences I had on that trip may be the closest I'll ever get to knowing what it was like to follow Jesus as His first disciples did. What was it like to follow Jesus in the flesh? What do you think His followers thought and felt when they first realized they were standing in the presence of the Son of God? Can you imagine sitting at the same table and eating with Him, hanging on His every word as He revealed the true meaning of the Scriptures?

The apostle John described that experience in this way:

That which was from the beginning, which we have heard, which we have seen with our eyes, which we looked upon and touched with our hands, concerning the word of life—the life was made manifest, and we have seen it, and testify to it and proclaim to you the eternal life, which was with the Father and was made manifest to us—that which we have seen and heard we proclaim also to you (1 John 1:1–3).

Many years later, the beloved John was still struck by the experience of seeing for himself the Word who was made flesh, looking at Jesus, and even touching Him with human hands. At various times in my life, I have thought, *Jesus, it would be amazing if You were still here in the flesh, and I could follow You, physically walk with You, see Your body language, watch how You deal with earthly life, and hear You say just the right thing in response to people who oppose You.* My imagination doesn't carry me very far until I remember what Jesus told His followers:

Nevertheless, I tell you the truth: it is to your advantage that I go away, for if I do not go away, the Helper will not come to you. But if I go, I will send him to you. And when he comes, he will convict the world concerning sin and righteousness and judgment (John 16:7–8).

THE PARACLETE—YOUR HELPER

The Greek word *paraclētos,* or in English *Paraclete,* is often translated 'Helper.' This word means someone who comes alongside another person, like a partner. It describes someone who will be right there with you to help, guide, and lead you. If you're a golfer, you might think of a caddy. Or if you are a mountain climber, you might think of someone like a Sherpa, the person who will carry your pack and help you get to the top of Mount Everest. The Holy Spirit is the One who advises you, helps you, and guides you. He's the One who knows the way to get you from where you are now to the place you need to go.

> *He's the One who knows the way to get you from where you are now to the place you need to go.*

Jesus used the word *Paraclete* to tell His followers about the One who would come to comfort, encourage, help, lead, and guide them. In essence, Jesus told them: "It's actually better for you if I'm not here because when I go to the Father, I will send the Spirit of God. He's going to come to you as a Helper, as a Guide, and as a Leader. And if I don't go away, I can't send Him to you. I know we're enjoying doing life together. I'm with you, and you're with Me. But when I go, I will put My Spirit inside you so that He will be in you and not just with you as I have been (see John 16:5–15)."

Leading up to His death, burial, and resurrection, Jesus talked to His disciples more about the Holy Spirit than anything else. They wanted to talk about the Pharisees. They wanted to talk about their positions in God's Kingdom—who would be at God's right and left hands? They wanted to know who was going to be the most important when they ultimately received their thrones. But Jesus, knowing He was about to go to the cross and hand the baton of ministry off to the disciples, spent more time, energy, and vocabulary talking about the Holy Spirit.

The disciples said things like, "Look, Jesus, You keep talking about leaving. You can't leave. We need You. We've got spectacular plans. We're going to run the Romans out of here and set up the Kingdom of God. We have plans to fix everything that has gone wrong. We need you here because we are going to build this thing." Jesus responded, "No, you don't understand. I'm leaving." Mark wrote,

> And he began to teach them that the Son of Man must suffer many things and be rejected by the elders and the chief priests and the scribes and be killed, and after three days rise again (Mark 8:31).

The disciples heard Him, but they weren't really listening. It's as if they were begging, "Jesus, You can't leave us!" The apostle Peter, ever ready to be their spokesperson, even took Jesus aside and scolded Him: "Far be it from you, Lord! This shall never happen to you" (Matthew 16:22).

Peter's words did not go over well with Jesus:

> [Jesus] turned and said to Peter, "Get behind me, Satan! You are a hindrance to me. For you are not setting your mind on the things of God, but on the things of man" (v. 23).

Peter didn't become Satan, but his words were straight "devil talk," and Jesus confronted him about it. Jesus knew what He had to do, and ultimately John 16:7–8 encapsulates what He wanted to say: "It's to your advantage that I go way."

ANOTHER LIKE HIMSELF

In Jesus' statement about the *Paraclete,* He conveyed an important quality about the One He was sending: the Holy Spirit, the One who comes alongside us, has the same quality and likeness as Jesus. Jesus was saying the Holy Spirit is not secondary to Him, nor is the Spirit of a lower class. The Church councils could affirm that the Spirit is not less God than Jesus is; that the Holy Spirit *is* God.

> *The Holy Spirit, the One who comes alongside us, has the same quality and likeness as Jesus.*

Though the first disciples didn't understand it at the time, Jesus was promising to send a Person of the Godhead to live and work within them. Their bodies would become the temple of the Holy Spirit, whom they would receive from God (see 1 Corinthians 6:19). In their pleas for Jesus not to leave them, the disciples were right about one thing: they knew they needed Jesus. To keep His promise not to leave them "as orphans" (see John 14:18), Jesus assured them He would send the Helper "who proceeds from the Father." The Holy Spirit would "bear witness" about Jesus, so they would not be left comfortless or without help (see John 15:26).

NEITHER LEFT NOR FORSAKEN

In Acts 2, Jesus' disciples received the infilling of the Holy Spirit. Just as Jesus had promised, He sent the Helper to bear witness about Him. Immediately, the Holy Spirit's presence manifested in the lives of the people in the early church, giving them a fresh understanding of the gospel, empowering them for service, granting them supernatural boldness to be witnesses in Jerusalem and beyond, and perhaps most importantly, enabling them to endure the harshest of persecutions for the gospel's sake.

And persecution did come their way. When the disciples willingly committed to following Jesus, it was not as if He told them, "You're going to have your best life ever." Instead, Jesus warned them that they could expect to be tested and mistreated just as He was.

> A disciple is not above his teacher, nor a servant above his master. It is enough for the disciple to be like his teacher, and the servant like his master. If they have called the master of the house Beelzebul, how much more will they malign those of his household (Matthew 10:24–25).

As the apostle Paul later would say, "Indeed, all who desire to live a godly life in Christ Jesus will be persecuted" (2 Timothy 3:12). For 300 years, Christians led neither revolts nor uprisings. Instead, they peacefully followed Jesus' example, and for doing so, they were persecuted by the most powerful empire in the world at that time—Rome.

From Jesus' crucifixion until Constantine's Edict of Toleration, Christians in the Roman Empire suffered through no less than 10 major persecutions.[1] Hundreds of thousands of Christians died as martyrs, the ultimate witness to their faith and commitment to Jesus. Their persecutors fed them to wild animals, burned them alive, removed their skin, and harmed their husbands, wives, or children in their presence. Many times, these Christians had the option to renounce Christ and offer burning incense on an altar recognizing the emperor as a god. So when Paul wrote, "No one can say 'Jesus is Lord' except in the Holy Spirit" (1 Corinthians 12:3), he was making a countercultural, politically dangerous statement. Confessing "Jesus is Lord" also implied "Caesar is not!"

As a reward for their faithfulness, Christians lost their livelihoods and businesses. They were often on the run from Roman authorities and unruly mobs. Christians were beaten, tortured, and even killed for their faith in the One true Lord, Jesus Christ. Paul himself suffered persecution at the hands of the Romans, the pagans, *and* Jewish leaders as he tried to preach Jesus as the Messiah.

How did severe persecution affect the body of Christ? It made her stronger in the Holy Spirit. The Church became even more dependent upon the Spirit for survival. Persecution served as a spiritual olive in the lives of Jesus' followers; through the process of crushing, it released the most valuable part of the fruit. Today's Christians have the great privilege of standing on the shoulders of those first believers and having a written record of their courageous acts. The early church walked in the power of the Holy Spirit, living in partnership with Him, just as Jesus did. How did that relationship show itself in the lives of those early believers? The book of Acts records the early church healing the sick, raising the dead, enduring rejection, and proclaiming the promise of the Holy Spirit for all believers—all in the name of Jesus.

In Acts 2 Peter addressed the crowd of people from around the world who had assembled in Jerusalem. Gathered in the upper room, a company of about 120 people had waited and prayed for the Holy Spirit to come. They did not know how He would first appear to them, but they were obedient to the instructions Jesus gave before He ascended into heaven. So they waited and waited.

> And suddenly there came from heaven a sound like a mighty rushing wind, and it filled the entire house where they were sitting. And divided tongues as of fire appeared to them and rested on each one of them. And they were all filled with the Holy Spirit and began to speak in other tongues as the Spirit gave them utterance (Acts 2:2–4).

From the street, the people who witnessed these events heard a cacophony of noise, which caused them to talk among themselves. They asked how it was possible for them to hear the praises of God spoken in their own languages (vv. 6–13).

Standing with the other disciples, Peter began to tell the crowd about what they were seeing and hearing. He ended his explanation with these words:

> Repent and be baptized every one of you in the name of Jesus Christ for the forgiveness of your sins, and you will receive the gift of the Holy Spirit. For the promise is for you and for your

children and for all who are far off, everyone whom the Lord our God calls to himself (Acts 2:38–39).

Once again, Jesus kept the promises He had made to His disciples. He told them He would be killed, and the Romans executed Him on a cross as a criminal. Jesus told His followers He would rise again, and in three days He was resurrected from death. He promised He would not leave them comfortless, and He did not, for He sent them the *Paraclete*. The beauty of all Jesus' kept promises, as Peter declared, is that same promise is now available for us today and all "who are afar off." Jesus sent the Helper after He returned to the Father, connecting us to Him through the Person of the Holy Spirit who now indwells us. And He will continue to give the *Paraclete* to every single believer, including you and me—as many as will call upon the name of the Lord.

Jesus, thank You for not leaving us without comfort. Thank You for sending Your Holy Spirit to us. We willingly choose to surrender to You and to give You our lives. We trust Your character. You always keep Your promises, and You watch over Your Word to perform it. We open our hearts and lives to the gift of the Holy Spirit. Empower us now to become Your witnesses to the whole world. In Jesus' name, Amen.

STUDY GUIDE

JESUS' DISCIPLES HAD THE UNIQUE, incredible experience of being in the physical presence of the incarnate Son of God. They were able to talk with Him, learn from Him, and even sit and eat meals with Him. When that experience ended following Jesus' death, resurrection, and ascension into heaven, God sent the Holy Spirit as the Helper to shepherd the disciples through the trials and persecutions to come.

REVIEW

1. How did the physical presence of Jesus affect those closest to Him? How did the disciples' fear of losing His presence manifest itself?
2. In what ways is it an advantage to have the Holy Spirit in the life of a believer as compared to just being with Jesus personally?
3. How were Christians treated for the first several centuries of the early church? How did the comfort and indwelling of the Spirit manifest itself in spite of the many persecutions they faced?

REFLECTION

1. How do you think you would have acted and responded to being in the presence of Jesus during His ministry?

2. What does it mean to you that the Holy Spirit is a Helper? What do you have to do to enable Him to help you?
3. In what ways are the promises of Jesus, as fulfilled at Pentecost, available to you today? How can you take advantage of those promises?

CHAPTER 3

YOUR CONNECTION

But you were washed, you were sanctified, you were justified in the name of the Lord Jesus Christ and by the Spirit of our God.

—The apostle Paul in 1 Corinthians 6:11

COULD ANYTHING BE MORE socially challenging than the initial moments of a first date? How do you behave? Should you shake hands? Then you have to figure out what to talk about. It's painfully awkward. First dates would be so much easier if they were not ... well, first dates!

Here's one of the wonderful things about the Holy Spirit: long before you were introduced to Him—way before your "first date"—He knew you and customized the Father's plan to reach you. In fact, the Holy Spirit was at work in your life well ahead of you ever giving Him a thought. That's pretty mind-blowing when you think about it, yet it's comforting too. It's as if you didn't have to ask God to move in your life, because He was already moving. He was already working, initiating how the Father would draw you to Jesus.

Jesus said people would not be able to come to Him unless the Father drew or granted them to come (see John 6:44, 65). He also said, " No one comes to the Father except through me" (John 14:6). In this divine dance of the Father drawing us to His Son and the Son making a way for us to the Father, we often overlook the role of the Holy Spirit. The Holy Spirit is the One who works at the bidding of the Father, inviting us to the dance, as it were. In this way, the Holy Spirit establishes a personal connection between us and God—Father, Son, and Holy Spirit.

There are numerous ways to respond and cooperate with the Holy Spirit in our ongoing partnership with Him, and I will address those ways in the next chapter. However, He is also actively involved in every facet of our lives as believers, doing things in us, for us, and through us even when we aren't aware of it. Often we will look back on events in our lives and realize God was at work. We didn't know it at the time, but He was definitely acting before we could even think about asking. Consider some of the following ways the Holy Spirit works in your life.

HE MAKES FIRST CONTACT WITH US

In the previous chapter, I wrote about the time Jesus told His disciples the Holy Spirit "will convict the world concerning sin and righteousness and judgment" (John 16:8). According to Jesus, this action is what the Holy Spirit does when we first encounter Him. He is the One who initiates contact with us. The Holy Spirit is our first contact.

The Holy Spirit is our first contact.

Following the Father's bidding, the Holy Spirit draws us to Jesus and simultaneously convicts us of our sin. For me, this experience happened when I was moving from childhood into adolescence. When I stayed with my grandparents, they faithfully took me to church with them whenever the doors were open. They were very godly people and had a great influence on me. My grandfather was the person who taught me to love the Bible. When I was a boy, he pulled me onto his lap in the mornings and read the Bible to me before he went to work. I remember his King James Version *Dickson Analytical Study Bible*; I thought it was huge, and I still do. It was as thick as a city phonebook with gold page-edging. I'm grateful to have that Bible. Sometimes I can still hear Grandpa reading the Bible and singing old hymns and choruses under his breath. He constantly sang worship songs. Watching him worship and leading others in worship at church are some of my earliest recollections. Those are good memories for me. Though I didn't know it at the time, what I was sensing was the presence of the Holy Spirit.

In the earliest years of my life, even before I could remember, my father chose to leave my mother. While she reared me by herself, my dad floated in and out of my life. Whenever he came around, he often exposed me to some of the things that wreaked havoc in his own life. Drugs, alcohol, and pornography were common factors in his life. My mother maintained a real faith, although she had lapsed a bit for a time. Our church attendance became sporadic. By the time I was 12, I had a lot of pain because of my father's inconsistent involvement in my life. I was hurting because he had exposed me to his negative behaviors. I was also experiencing some painful abuse and bullying from other kids in my neighborhood, all while trying to cope with my debilitating shyness and insecurity. I am thankful that my grandparents were a consistent part of my life, and they influenced me greatly toward the Lord.

One Sunday night during a summer visit, my grandfather told me to get ready for church. I really wanted to stay at the house and play baseball, but he said, "It's Sunday night, and on Sunday nights, we go to church!" I begrudgingly climbed into their little Plymouth Horizon, and we drove to Good Shepherd Assembly of God in Clarkston, Michigan. I don't remember anything remarkable about that particular service. I can't tell you which songs were sung or what the pastor preached about. What I do remember is that I was drawing on the inside of one of the hymnals, just trying to pass the time until the service ended. (I know it was naughty, but I'm being honest.)

At the service drew near to a close, the pastor issued a call for everyone to move to the front of the auditorium to pray. Now as a 12-year-old boy, I thought that was one of the worst things you could do. This was not a young congregation—I was the youngest person there by about five decades that night. Even so, I got up from my seat and made my way to the front with all the adults. The pastor told us to form a circle, and then everyone began to pray. Well, everyone *but* me. I was passing the time trying to discern pictures and patterns in the brown, rust, and cream-colored stains formed from old roof leaks above the ceiling tiles. What I didn't know was that I was about to have a personal encounter with the Holy Spirit.

Something began to happen as I stood in the front of that church. I immediately started to experience what I believe was some kind of trance. I was physically present with all the people in the prayer circle, but in another way I had stepped into a divine encounter with the Lord. He began to show me all the pieces to my life's story—all of the painful experiences, the feelings of abandonment, and the hurts and fears I felt but didn't know how to process or even talk about. He was laying all of these things out for me to see, and somehow in the presence of the Lord, I saw Him weaving them together into something new and hopeful. I heard the Lord speak my name in what I thought was an audible voice. It was comforting. Then I heard Him tell me that He was calling me and setting me apart to be a voice for Him to my generation.

Suddenly, in that moment, the Lord took away all the guilt, shame, and pain I had carried into the church building. He filled me with a new sense that my life had meaning—that I wasn't a mistake. Before that moment, I had already grown sensitive to the things of God and the Holy Spirit, and I give my grandparents the credit for their influence. But there, at the front of that church, I had my first recognizable contact with the Holy Spirit. From that moment on, He placed within me a hunger and a thirst for God's presence, which forever changed my life.

After several intense yet comforting minutes, I once again gained an awareness of my surroundings. It was only then I realized that no one else had witnessed what I had just experienced. It was only for me. I had received a real and personal visit from none other than the Holy Spirit. The living God my grandfather read to me about in the Bible knew my name, and He wanted me to hear His voice and know just what He thought about me. I admit it was completely overwhelming.

As I look back on that night, I recognize all of us have different stories about the times God has met with us. Some of them are not as dramatic as the two disciples' road to Emmaus encounter or Paul's experience on the road to Damascus. However, they are all just as real. The kind of wonder that causes us to respond with worship shows us that God can and will customize His visitations so He can give us exactly what we need when we need it. He will convict and draw each of us through His Holy Spirit in the most perfect way for us individually. Can you see that the Creator of the universe has personally considered *you?* He knows what is best for you, how to reveal Himself to you, and when He will do it for you.

God can and will customize His visitations so He can give us exactly what we need when we need it.

English poet Francis Thompson (1859–1907) once penned a poem entitled "Hound of Heaven." In it, he depicted God in relentless pursuit of the sinner. It is a vivid picture of the role of the Holy Spirit and His breathless hunt to unleash His gracious work in our lives. My friend, God is letting loose the Hound of Heaven on you. His intention is not to harm you. In His passionate love for you, He wants to make first contact, pull you away from sin, and draw you to the heart of Jesus.

HE REGENERATES US

Once the Holy Spirit makes contact with us, the next thing He does is *regenerate* us when we are born again in Jesus. One night a man named Nicodemus met secretly with Jesus. This is what Jesus said to him:

> Truly, truly, I say to you, unless one is born again he cannot see the kingdom of God.... Truly, truly I say to you, unless one is born of water and the Spirit, he cannot enter the kingdom of God. That which is born of the flesh is flesh, and that which is born of the Spirit is spirit. Do not marvel that I said to you, "You must be born again." The wind blows where it wishes, and you hear its sound, but you do not know where it comes from or where it goes. So it is with everyone who is born of the Spirit (John 3:3, 5–8).

When Jesus told Nicodemus that he must be born again, He was saying that Nicodemus needed to be regenerated. What does this mean? If you are reading this book, then you are physically alive, but that does not mean you are spiritually alive (although I pray that you are or soon will be). The apostle Paul made this fact very clear when he told the Ephesians that although they were physically alive, they were dead in their trespasses and sins before salvation (see Ephesians 2:1). Prior to coming to faith, we have our souls, which include our minds and instincts, and we have our physical bodies. Nevertheless, we do not have spiritual life inside of us before we believe in Jesus by faith. Put simply, we are spiritually dead. For us to become spiritually alive, then, something must transpire. This is what is called regeneration.

Re- means "again." *Generate* means "to give life." Regeneration is the process of giving life again or being born again.

As I said previously, the Holy Spirit draws us to Jesus and convicts us of sin. Jesus then puts His Holy Spirit in us. In the Old Testament, *ruach* is the only Hebrew word used to mean *wind, breath,* and *spirit.* In Genesis 1, God formed Adam and then breathed into his nostrils. That is the point when Adam became a living being or living soul. That word translated *breath* there is the same word rendered as *spirit* and *wind.*

In the New Testament there is also one word translated *wind, breath,* and *spirit,* and it is *pneuma.* So when Jesus talked to Nicodemus about the wind in John 3, He used the very same word that is translated *spirit* or *breath.* Consider the implications of this word. When we receive the Spirit, it's as if God breathes directly from His mouth into our nostrils, just as He did with Adam at the creation of all humanity. By breathing into us or in-spiriting us, He gives us life, and we become spiritually alive! This life is not one you can earn or purchase. You cannot manufacture it through your own efforts. Only God can give it to you. If you place your faith in Jesus Christ, then you have life infused into you by the living God. It's as if you have been born all over again—like you're an infant, a new child of the Spirit.

When God breathed His life into your dead spirit, He gave you *His* life. He in-spirited you with life that is eternal in its nature and will never go away. Like Adam, God created you once as flesh. Now in Christ, you are born the second time of the Spirit, and that is how He regenerates you. He gives you new life. The apostle Paul writes,

He saved us, not because of works done by us in righteousness, but according to his own mercy, by the washing of regeneration and renewal of the Holy Spirit, whom he poured out on us richly through Jesus Christ our Savior (Titus 3:5–6).

Through regeneration, the Holy Spirit is acting, and He is the agent. For everything God creates, He is the One who determines it within Himself as God the Father. He speaks it as God the Son (Jesus, the Word). And He executes it as God the Holy Spirit. Just as the Holy Spirit was hovering over the deep and just as He was hovering over Mary's womb, the Holy Spirit has now been sent into the world to convict it of sin, righteousness, and judgment. When we turn to the Lord and recognize our own sin and guilt, we place our faith in Jesus' finished work on the cross. Then what happens? The same Holy Spirit recreates a spirit—a living life eternal in nature—inside us.

> *When we turn to the Lord and recognize our own sin and guilt, we place our faith in Jesus' finished work on the cross.*

This is what Jesus means when He says we must be "born again." Becoming a Christian isn't merely arriving at a mental decision or developing a code of ethics. Believers do not say, "Oh, I believe that I'm the same person I always was, but I now also believe in Jesus and want to apply His ethics to my life." No, you can't come to Him unless the Spirit draws and convicts you, and you cannot remain the same because the Holy Spirit regenerates you, making you into a brand new person who now is spiritually alive. The apostle Paul reminds us, "If anyone is in Christ, he is a new creation. The old has passed away; behold, the new has come" (2 Corinthians 5:17). You actually *are* a new creation, because through His Holy Spirit, God has created a new work inside of you.

HE FREES US

The Holy Spirit brings us into freedom. Let's read once again what Jesus declared as His mission statement and job description:

> The Spirit of the Lord is upon me,
>> because he has anointed me
>> to proclaim good news to the poor.
> He has sent me to proclaim liberty to the captives
>> and recovering of sight to the blind,
>> to set at liberty those who are oppressed (Luke 4:18).

Jesus made it clear that the Spirit of the Lord proclaims liberty (freedom). The apostle Paul later affirmed this idea when he wrote, "Now the Lord is the Spirit, and where the Spirit of the Lord is, there is freedom" (2 Corinthians 3:17).

The Holy Spirit and freedom are mutually inclusive. Why is this true? Consider the nature of bondage and the characteristics of captivity. Bondage is the result of being ensnared. Captivity happens when we've been trapped. Bondage and captivity are outside of God's design and will for our lives. When He confronts those traps in our lives, what do you suppose happens? Do you think God gives up and yields to those things that stand against His design and will, or do those things have to surrender to Him? My experience tells me everything that is not part of His will and design must one day surrender to Him. Whenever Jesus encountered things that were outside His will, those things changed. But He didn't change.

We live in a tension between "now" and "not yet." We live now as people of the Kingdom of God, and ultimately, we are citizens of heaven. We have eternity dwelling inside us, yet we know we still live in a fallen and broken world until Jesus comes back. Even now, we are surrounded by sin, death, destruction, poverty, racism, and other things we know are not submitted to the will of God. Furthermore, God has called us to be in partnership with Jesus as earthly agents who pray for His will to be accomplished on the earth as it is in heaven. We know that everything on the earth will be made right when Jesus comes back.

Because we live in a world where things are not as they're supposed to be, we experience some knots that tie us up. Sometimes we become ensnared by those knots, and that is what bondage is. Things become tangled, and we get trapped in false belief systems that we mistake for truth. Those false systems may include paradigms, fears, doubts, insecurities, or even religious traditions. However, the Good News is that Jesus said the Holy Spirit would be our Leader, our Guide, our Comforter, and our Truth Teller. His truth sets us free. The Spirit brings greater levels and understanding of freedom as we surrender to Him.

HE SANCTIFIES US

The Holy Spirit *sanctifies* us. I recognize the word *sanctify* is not a term commonly used today, even in the Church. We don't talk about the concept of sanctification enough, largely because many people don't understand it. Instead, we talk about salvation, because we understand it and know what it means to "be saved." Many of us can remember how the Reverend Billy Graham preached about salvation like nobody else could, and stadiums full of people responded by streaming into the aisles to reach the altar in the front. I'm still hoping and believing for new days when stadiums will once again be filled and altars will be full with tens of thousands of people just as they were during those Crusades.

So yes, we talk a lot about salvation. But I am here to tell you that sanctification is just as much a part of the work of the Holy Spirit in the life of a believer as salvation is. Obviously, we know salvation is a defining moment that starts and finishes when the Holy Spirit works in us, draws us to Jesus, convicts us of sin, regenerates us, and sets us free.

> *Sanctification is just as much a part of the work of the Holy Spirit in the life of a believer as salvation is.*

Sanctification then becomes the ongoing work of the Holy Spirit in our lives. He is actively conforming us into the image of Jesus. For us to understand sanctification, we must avoid either of two extremes. I remember my grandfather saying, "For every one mile of truth, there are two miles of error. And there's a ditch on either side." Using that homespun analogy, understand that there are those on one side of the road who believe, "Well, once we get saved, we should have perfect and sinless lives from that point on." The theological term for that way of thinking is *perfectionism,* and it was a part of the pietist and holiness movements. Perfectionism is the idea that believers would first experience salvation and then have a second experience in which the Holy Spirit would burn away all desire for sin, giving believers pure and perfect hearts. For pietists, sanctification is an event instead of an ongoing and progressive process. Some Christians, even today, have adopted a holiness perspective that says, "I have been sanctified," which means they have reached a state of moral perfection in which they no longer sin.

On the other side of the theological road is another group of people who say, "We prayed the prayer. We are saved by grace, so now it doesn't matter what we do or how we live because nothing we do can affect or change that. We are sinners who have been saved by grace. We're never going to change. We don't need to grow. If anything goes wrong, we have our insurance policy, our salvation." If you subscribe to this viewpoint, then there is no need to see any growth or change take place in your life because you think salvation is the only measure that matters. You may even think that any talk about holiness nullifies God's gift of grace.

The truth, however, is that the Bible talks about sanctification as a progressive, ongoing work of the Holy Spirit in our lives.

His ultimate goal is to conform us into the image of Christ Jesus. To *sanctify* something means to it make it holy. You may remember those popular bracelets from the 1990s that asked, "W.W.J.D.?" ("What Would Jesus Do?"). Sanctification not only asks, "What would Jesus do?" but also "What *is* Jesus doing?" These are the questions we are called to ask, and we are to listen as the Holy Spirit provides the answers. He wants to change us from the inside out so that we will begin to do the things Jesus does rather than the old things we used to do before we were saved.

I will also say that the Holy Spirit is good at sanctifying us. He is good and patient. He's kind yet firm. The Holy Spirit is shaping and forming us to be more and more like Jesus. His sanctification is a silent work in our lives, and we are often unaware of what He is doing. We don't always understand that what we're going through is molding us and making us to be holy as Jesus is holy. In the difficult seasons of life, you may wonder, *Why am I going through this?* There can be more than one answer to that question. Perhaps the devil is trying to harm or harass you. I am a firm believer in spiritual warfare, and the devil deserves a lot of blame. At times, you may have to admit that you've brought difficulties on yourself, or someone else could be doing something to affect you negatively out of their own misguided free will. Even with all of those possibilities, I know the Holy Spirit wants to use every difficult situation to shape, define, and form you to become more like Jesus.

The Holy Spirit may not be the cause of a difficulty, but you can be sure that He will take advantage of it. The apostle Paul recognized this truth when he wrote, "We know that for those who love God all things work together for good, for those who are called according to his purpose" (Romans 8:28). I know people often misquote this verse and say, "All things are going to work out good." The Bible doesn't say that. It says God is working all things *for* your good. It doesn't mean He's going to make all things good.

There are times when the Holy Spirit will use some pretty bad experiences to bring about some pretty good purposes in our lives. Sometimes He uses some painful things. Like a chisel in the hands of a master sculptor, He will use these experiences to chip away at the granite of our lives so He can expose a masterpiece hidden inside. Paul reminds us that you and I are God's masterpieces, "his workmanship, created in Christ Jesus for good works" (Ephesians 2:10).

So I will say again, the Holy Spirit sanctifies us. He is always working in us and for our good. It's crucial for us to understand this truth because far too often we think about God as Father and God as Son, but we forget He is also the Holy Spirit. When we have a proper understanding of the Holy Spirit and His work, we know that every moment of every day God is with us and working in us through His Holy Spirit. Whether you recognize it or not, there has never been a moment in your life as a believer when the Holy Spirit was not working in you for your benefit.

There has never been a moment in your life as a believer when the Holy Spirit was not working in you for your benefit.

43

HE SEALS US

The Holy Spirit *seals us* on the day of our salvation. This is how the apostle Paul explained the significance of that action:

> In him you also, when you heard the word of truth, the gospel of your salvation, and believed in him, were sealed with the promised Holy Spirit, who is the guarantee of our inheritance until we acquire possession of it, to the praise of his glory (Ephesians 1:13–14).

Notice some of the words in this verse, such as *guarantee, inheritance*, and *possession*. All of these words are wrapped around the image of a seal. Paul was telling the Ephesian believers that the Holy Spirit acts as the seal (the guarantee) of their inheritance. A seal has traditionally served as the guarantee of a legal document. For example, your birth certificate must bear a proper seal for it to be considered legitimate in the eyes of your local Department of Motor Vehicles (DMV) or any passport agency.

The Roman Empire required legal documents to bear proper seals to be deemed authentic. For example, a first-century father who wanted to leave an inheritance to his son had to go to a lawyer to draw up the will. Once completed, the father had to approve the will. The lawyer then rolled the document into a scroll and poured melted wax on the edge of the scroll for two seals to be placed. The first seal was pressed into the wax by the father, as he was the one bequeathing the inheritance. He would take his signet ring, which served as his authentic signature or brand, and press it firmly into the hot wax, thus sealing the will. This seal was not to be broken until the time came for the will to be probated. The attorney impressed the second seal, which served as his attestation that he oversaw the will's creation. If the father had a large estate or inheritance to leave to his son, or if the father were a member of the royal or noble family, then a third seal was required. This seal would come from the emperor himself.

The will with all its seals would be given as a gift to the son on the day of his wedding as a statement of the transference of wealth from one generation to the next. The father intended the gift to enable the son to start his own family with confidence for the future. In essence, the gift was the father's way of saying, "You're starting your own home, and this is your inheritance. Your future is secure."

Of course, the son wouldn't open the will immediately once it was given to him; that would be presumptuous, at best. He knew he was expected to keep it until the appointed day after his father died. Following the wedding, the son would continue to work, helping build his father's business. The will gave the son confidence that the business or property wouldn't be given to somebody else; it was his, and he had it. He just couldn't receive all the property declared in the will because the father was still present. However, the son had the sure guarantee of his father, the lawyer, and sometimes even the emperor, because it was sealed by all of them.

Though the son had yet to open the will to read it, he knew its contents. When the father eventually died, the seals were then broken and the document read in front of the family. If the will had public implications, then it was read aloud by the same lawyer who had crafted it so that everyone would understand what was being transferred to the son's ownership and possession.

Once again, consider what Paul wrote in Ephesians 1:13–14. He said the Holy Spirit seals you, which means it is as if the Father has taken your inheritance and marked it as belonging to you. That means everything belongs to you. The Kingdom belongs to you. Salvation belongs to you, as well as eternal life and the ultimate redemption of your body. If you are in Christ, then there is an inheritance for you in the Kingdom of God.

Right now, however, you have not realized your full inheritance. In this world, you don't experience the ultimate redemption of your body. You only see in part, and you experience in part. Yes, we see healings break in. God performs miracles, but those are only a foretaste of the age to come. This foretaste of the Kingdom and the truth of God's Word tell us a day is coming when the full redemption of our bodies will take place. Like that first-century son, you have received the promise of your inheritance that will one day be fully revealed. At the moment of your conversion, the Holy Spirit sealed your inheritance, and you became a full-blown son or daughter of your heavenly Father.

You now hold the promise, and you carry it here on earth and in your heart. The Holy Spirit has sealed you, and He is given to you as a reminder of what truly belongs to you, both now and in the future. There is coming a day when Jesus will return, when the scrolls will be opened, and your full inheritance in the Kingdom of God will be read. The apostle John wrote about this wonderful day in the future:

Beloved, we are God's children now, and what we will be has not yet appeared; but we know that when he appears we shall be like him, because we shall see him as he is (1 John 3:2).

He is given to you as a reminder of what truly belongs to you, both now and in the future.

When Jesus comes back, I don't think our minds can conceive the glory that is to be revealed in and through Him. We get little hints. Did you know that Paul even wrote that a day will come when you and I will judge angels (see 1 Corinthians 6:3)? Isn't that incredible? There is no way we can have a full understanding of who we are as sons and daughters of God. Even the angels of heaven will look at us and say, "She is a daughter of God" or "He is a son of God." Even they know we are a work in development. We are maturing, and one day we will reign with Jesus. Our bodies are aging in this sin-contaminated world, but the Holy Spirit lives inside us, and the angels recognize it. They know we are marked by God, who put His own Spirit on us and in us as the guarantee of our glorious inheritance that is to come.

One day, Jesus will be fully revealed. All the world will see Him, and all of heaven will witness the revelation and full manifestation of the sons and daughters of God. We will emerge from the grave, glorified just like Jesus, and receive our full inheritance. The Kingdom will come, and we will reign and rule forever with Him. It will be a magnificent day! But for now, God has sealed us with the promise of the Holy Spirit. He is the guarantee that we will receive our inheritance!

Father, we are thankful that You have revealed Yourself to us in Jesus Christ. Thank You for winning our hearts and giving us new life and hope through the resurrection of Your Son. We are forever grateful for all You have done for us. Give us hearts that are open, receptive, and hungry for everything You have for us.

Holy Spirit, speak to us. Increase our understanding. Teach us how to partner with You, walking in step with You every moment of the day. In Jesus' name, Amen.

STUDY GUIDE

THE HOLY SPIRIT invites us to into a relationship with God the Father through Jesus the Son. He will make contact with you in a way that is unique for you. The Spirit then regenerates you when you are born again. He sets you free and removes the bondage of sin from your life. His sanctification is a progressive, ongoing work in your life. The Holy Spirit seals you with the guarantee of an eternal inheritance, in which all believers will reign and rule forever with Jesus.

REVIEW

1. How did the Holy Spirit manifest Himself to me in that small church when I was 12 years old? What are some other manifestations we read about in the New Testament?
2. What words in the Old and New Testaments are translated *wind*, *breath*, and *spirit*? How does God the Father activate Himself in our spirits?
3. What does it mean that the Holy Spirit sanctifies us? What are different ways the process of sanctification has been understood in the Church?

REFLECTION

1. How has the Holy Spirit made contact with you in your life? How did you respond?

2. What does it mean to you for the Holy Spirit to recreate a living, spiritual life inside you?
3. Have you been sanctified, set free, and sealed with the Holy Spirit? If not, what is holding you back from accepting that promise?

CHAPTER 4

YOUR PARTNER

For what we proclaim is not ourselves, but Jesus Christ as Lord, with ourselves as your servants for Jesus' sake. For God, who said, "Let light shine out of darkness," has shone in our hearts to give the light of the knowledge of the glory of God in the face of Jesus Christ.

But we have this treasure in jars of clay, to show that the surpassing power belongs to God and not to us.

—The apostle Paul in 2 Corinthians 4:5–7

YOU'VE HEARD THE SAYING, "Confession is good for the soul," right? Well, I have a confession: I was kicked out of Bible college. Now, before you jump to the conclusion that I committed a crazy, sophomoric prank or some jail-deserving crime, let me explain. I was asked to leave because I believed and professed that God still speaks and does miracles. Let that sink in for a moment.

The college's leadership didn't want to have a theology graduate from their school who didn't believe like they did. I was in shock. For the first time in my life, I met Christians who were actually angry with me for saying that God still talks to us and works miracles in our lives through His great power. I wonder what they would think if they knew I was advocating that the Holy Spirit wants to partner with us in our everyday lives!

The writer of Hebrews says that the new covenant Jesus mediates is "much more excellent than the old" (Hebrews 8:6).

What he means is that the new covenant is a superior one. How can we have a superior covenant if our communication, proximity, power, and access to God are inferior? The answer is we can't. The New Testament shows and promises an intimacy and partnership that require communication, proximity, power, access, revelation, direction, and much more. God provides these to us through our relationship with the Holy Spirit. They are the ways we partner with Him.

WE HAVE ACCESS

The Holy Spirit gives us real, intimate access to the Father. The apostle Paul writes, "For through him we both have access in one Spirit to the Father" (Ephesians 2:18). God does not intend for us to maintain religious traditions that relate to Him from a distance, as though we are here on earth and He is way up in the highest heavens. No, through Jesus, we have intimate and immediate access by way of the Holy Spirit.

The apostle John expresses that access in this way: "And by this we know that he abides in us, by the Spirit whom he has given us" (1 John 3:24; see also 4:13). Notice that John says this on two occasions in his first epistle, so he must have thought it was important. God dwells within us by the Holy Spirit, whom He gave to us. That same Spirit gives us intimate access to the Father. In their prayer lives, many people still struggle with the idea that they somehow have to get God's attention before they can do anything else. It is as if they think, "I'm here, and God is way up there." It is an important paradigm shift for us to realize that our hearts are now the Holy of Holies.

Jesus said, "If anyone loves me, he will keep my word, and my Father will love him, and we will come to him and make our home with him" (John 14:23). The way God abides in us is through the Holy Spirit, which means you and I have constant, complete, and unhindered access to the Father at all times. You don't have to *get* God's attention; you *have* His attention! So if you experience a block in communication with God, then it's likely on your end and not His.

Distractions, fear, busyness, sin, and shame are all things that can keep us from an intimate relationship and fellowship with God if we allow them to do so. Perhaps you have thought God was a bit put off by your requests or standoffish toward you for something you thought you did or didn't do. If so, then you won't take advantage of the access to the Father that the Holy Spirit has given you. If you feel as if God doesn't want to hear you, or you think you are bothering Him too much with your needs and constant petitions, then you do not have a true understanding of who He is.

I really want you to understand that you have immediate, open, and ongoing access to the Father through the Holy Spirit. As I mentioned in the introduction, the Holy Spirit is the imminent presence of God in us, personally making known the presence of God to us. Remember, the Holy Spirit is the closest Person of the Godhead for you to relate to on a daily, moment-to-moment basis. Everywhere you go, God goes, because He dwells in you. You take Him with you. If you are in the car, then He is there. When you are at work, He is there. As you lie down to sleep, He's there too. But He's also on that date you are having with someone you know you shouldn't be dating. The Holy Spirit is available to talk with you at any time. You can ask for His help, wisdom, knowledge, understanding, provision, and power because you have access to the Father through Him. And He will respond—He talks back. The Father still speaks to us, and He does it through His Word and by His Holy Spirit.

The Holy Spirit is the closest Person of the Godhead for you to relate to on a daily, moment-to-moment basis.

WE HAVE REVELATION

The Holy Spirit reveals Jesus' identity, will, and Word. Jesus said,

> When the Spirit of truth comes, he will guide you into all the truth, for he will not speak on his own authority, but whatever he hears he will speak, and he will declare to you the things that are to come. He will glorify me, for he will take what is mine and declare it to you (John 16:13–14).

Jesus also said the Holy Spirit "will teach [us] all things and bring to [our] remembrance all that I have said" (see John 14:26).

Notice the way Jesus framed what He said in John 16—"When the Spirit of truth comes." The Holy Spirit was sent to us as "the Spirit of truth." He perfectly knows Jesus (the Word) and the Father. Consequently, He has been given to us to reveal who Jesus is. The primary way He does this is through God's Word, the Bible.

People often act as if there is some competition between the Word and the Holy Spirit. I receive questions such as, "Well, are you a Word person or are a Spirit person? Are you a charismatic church or a Bible church?" The reality is that there is neither competition nor contradiction between the Word and the Spirit. The Holy Spirit is actually the One who inspired and gave the Word. No writer invented the Bible out of his own intellect or interpretation. In fact, the apostle Peter wrote, "Holy men of God spoke *as they were* moved by the Holy Spirit" (2 Peter 1:21 NKJV). So the Holy Spirit inspired those words. Yes, men wrote them down, but they did so under the inspiration of the Holy Spirit.

In fact, there is no conflict between the Word and the Spirit at all. The same Holy Spirit who inspired the Scriptures is the One who wants to illuminate and reveal Himself through those same words. He wants to disclose Himself to us over and over again in our lives so we can fully understand who Jesus is and grow to be more like Him.

Learning who Jesus is cannot be accomplished through a mere mental operation or just by giving assent to a set of facts. Jesus said, "You shall love the Lord your God with all your heart and with all your soul and with all your mind" (Matthew 22:37). We love God with both our minds and our spirits—they need not be in battle against one another. We will not learn who Jesus is simply by saying, "Holy Spirit, show me who Jesus is" and then waiting for the knowledge to sink into us through osmosis. We must partner with Him and seek Him through a passionate pursuit. As we read the Scripture, we must engage our minds and become diligent students of the Bible. However, I urge you not to read the Bible as only an intellectual exercise. Read it as a way to hear from the Holy Spirit so you can see things as He does. As you read the Bible, let your prayer be, "Holy Spirit, I want You to lift off the page those things I need to see so I can get a clearer picture of who Jesus is and what His will is for my life." If you pray in this way while reading the Bible, then the words and stories will come alive in a new and fresh way.

The Holy Spirit will highlight things you need to see as you read the Bible with Him. He will begin to craft a picture of who Jesus is. Now, you can't read the Bible one time and expect to know who Jesus is. You must read it over and over again. The Holy Spirit will paint on the canvas of your heart and mind the portraits and landscapes, illustrating those things that God has freely given to you. You have been given the Holy Spirit so that you can fully understand what God has given to you in Christ Jesus (1 Corinthians 2:12).

> *The Holy Spirit will highlight things you need to see as you read the Bible with Him.*

We must be students of God's Word. If you read the Bible as though it were a task on a religious checklist, then you will find it is boring and, for the most part, unprofitable. If, however, you know that God wants to reveal Himself through its Holy-Spirit-inspired pages, then you will begin to recognize that the Word and the Spirit are both indispensable gifts from God.

Spiritual hunger operates in a way that is precisely the opposite of physical hunger. Physical hunger occurs if you don't eat for an extended time. The longer you refrain from eating, the hungrier you'll become. Spiritual hunger has an opposite effect. The longer you stay away from consuming God's Word, the less you will crave it, and the more you will want to consume other things. Conversely, the more you consume God's Word, the more you will become hungry for it.

Have you always wanted to fall in love with the Bible but just can't figure out how to do so? Then start reading the Bible every day. If you do, then your appetite will only increase. Do you want to grow closer to the Holy Spirit? Then study the Holy Spirit. Dig deeper into the Him and you will develop an appetite for more of Him.

WE HAVE DIRECTION

The Holy Spirit is available to lead us. Just as He led Jesus into the wilderness (see Matthew 4:1), the Holy Spirit will lead and drive us if we submit to Him. The apostle Paul says, "All who are led by the Spirit of God are sons of God" (Romans 8:14).

God designed us as His children to operate in the most effective and efficient way we can according to Kingdom principles, which means we will be led by the Holy Spirit. Paul says that before we were born again, we were "by nature children of wrath," living "in the passions of our flesh, carrying out the desires of the body and the mind" (Ephesians 2:3). Once we have been regenerated, the Holy Spirit sets up residence inside of us, and we are no longer led by our passions or flesh.

As people who are born again, we are not led by our instincts or our lowest desires. Neither does God mean for us to be led by popular opinion. He wants us to be led by His Holy Spirit, just as Jesus was when He was led into the wilderness.

Sometimes God will lead you to a place you do not expect. If someone had told me 25 years ago that I would move to Kalamazoo, Michigan, then I would have said, "Oh, no. That's not God's will for my life. I'm a city guy." You see, I grew up in Grand Rapids. The only time I ever traveled to Kalamazoo was to go to Wing Stadium to see concerts with the Imperials and Petra. Those events were the only frame of reference I had for Kalamazoo. On Route 131, you would either travel south to Kalamazoo or north to Big Rapids. I was a Grand Rapids dude.

When my wife, Jane, and I began to experience the leading of the Holy Spirit to come to Kalamazoo, we started to become open and embrace His direction. I remember when we drove to Portage, Michigan, and we thought that was where all the action was. Was God leading us there? Next, we drove to Battle Creek, and we thought there was some action going on downtown, and maybe that's where the Holy Spirit wanted us to go.

Then, one day we were driving down a two-lane highway out in the middle of nowhere called *M-89* (Michigan 89). We came around the corner of the road, right in the middle of a cornfield, and I thought, *Oh, dear God, can we just keep going?* Then I heard the still, small voice of the Spirit say, "This is where I want you to start." I turned to tell Jane what I was experiencing, and before I could get the words out of my mouth, she said, "I think we're supposed to start here."

I wish I could tell you that I was excited by her words of immediate confirmation to what I had heard the Holy Spirit say. But no, I wasn't. My only thought was, *There is nothing here. God, I'm going to go crazy. You know I'm a city person. I grew up on Division Avenue next to the Log Cabin Bar and the Paragon Bowling Alley. I'm a Detroit kid!*

But I had been praying. I'd been telling God that I would do whatever He wanted me to do. I had said, "I will plant a church. Just don't make me pastor a small church with pews in a small town." And wouldn't you know, God wanted Jane and me to start a church from zero in a village. That's right, a village. According to the 2010 census, Richland is a village with a population of less than 1,000 people.[1] At least I can say that God answered my prayer about no pews!

Here is what you need to know: God will lead us according to His will and not our own. He knows the beginning from the end. Today, I am exceedingly grateful because I love my city. I love Richland, and I love Portage. I love the people. I love what God has done. I love the fact that He loves to start in the most difficult, obscure places and do something that astounds the wise. He even loves to astound us. It's as if God is saying, "You thought that was impossible? You thought I couldn't do that?" The older I become, the more I realize His work has nothing to do with the size of the community but everything to do with the size of the leader.

God needed to do so much work inside me, and He picked a beautiful place to do it. Sometimes we try to lead ourselves and make our own determinations about how things should go. However, God is not like us. He doesn't lead us according to human logic. God won't take a poll, and He rarely asks for our opinions. He has a plan, and He gave the Holy Spirit to lead us into that plan if we will partner with Him. If we pay attention to the Holy Spirit, then He will lead us in our everyday decisions. The Spirit wants to direct us in our conversations, including whom we should talk to. He wants to guide us as we share our faith. The Holy Spirit wants to steer us in our parenting. The Spirit is not so spiritual that He doesn't want to speak to us about very practical things.

The Holy Spirit wants to lead and guide us in every area of our lives. He knows the direction and will of the Father for our lives and destinies. Furthermore, He knows what needs to happen to get us there. Our job is to look to Him, listen to Him, and obey Him. Where He leads us, we want to follow.

WE HAVE AN INTERCESSOR

The Holy Spirit intercedes for us. Here are two of my favorite verses in the New Testament:

> Likewise the Spirit helps us in our weakness. For we do not know what to pray for as we ought, but the Spirit himself intercedes for us with groanings too deep for words. And he who searches hearts knows what is the mind of the Spirit, because the Spirit intercedes for the saints according to the will of God (Romans 8:26–27).

Do you realize that the Holy Spirit living in you is your great Prayer Partner? He understands everything that is going on inside you—body, soul, and spirit. And the Holy Spirit knows what the mind and will of God is for you. Therefore, He prays to the Father on your behalf with understanding and knowledge beyond your comprehension. And He intercedes with you.

Not only do you have the Holy Spirit praying for and with you, but you also have another Intercessor and Advocate. It's Jesus! He is sitting on the throne next to the Father. Jesus is constantly making intercession for you before the Father, and the Holy Spirit is constantly making intercession from the earth on your behalf. It is good to have Spirit-empowered, earthly intercessors who are praying for you as the Holy Spirit leads them. But you always have two much more powerful Intercessors. The Holy Spirit and Jesus always intercede on your behalf. Not only that, but the Holy Spirit also invites us to intercede with Him and Jesus for others. We can pray for the needs of our loved ones and strangers alike as the Holy Spirit places that concern in our hearts and prompts us. I will discuss more about this later, but it's wonderful to have the three-fold cord of agreement in prayer: your prayers, the Holy Spirit's prayers, and Jesus' prayers. It's truly amazing!

> *The Holy Spirit and Jesus always intercede on your behalf.*

WE HAVE POWER

The Holy Spirit empowers us. But for *what* does He empower us? The Spirit empowers us to serve and give witness. In Acts 1:8, Luke recorded Jesus' last words to His disciples. Jesus told them they would "receive power when the Holy Spirit has come upon you." He followed that promise by stating, "And you will be my witnesses in Jerusalem and in all Judea and Samaria, and to the end of the earth."

Jesus was telling the disciples that when the Holy Spirit came, He would manifest in power. The Spirit would empower the early church, just as He empowers you and me even now. In 1 Corinthians 12, the apostle Paul writes about the gifts of the Spirit, which I will unpack much more in a later chapter. It's interesting, though, that Paul says there are different gifts and operations, but it is the same Lord and the same Spirit who empowers those gifts in each of us (see 1 Corinthians 12:4–6).

The Holy Spirit was not given to you merely to be a silent partner who won't make Himself known and isn't available in your everyday life. No, the Holy Spirit wants to empower you for service in every sphere of your life. He is very practical and down to earth, and He especially wants to empower you to be His witness.

Jesus promised His followers that the Spirit would give them power to be witnesses, and one of the first evidences of the Spirit's presence in any believer's life is depicted in Acts 2:14–40. Peter boldly proclaimed the Word of God after receiving the Holy Spirit. Remember, just 50 days before, he denied even knowing Jesus! But under the power of the Holy Spirit, Peter spoke louder and bolder than anyone else. We need boldness. Being a Christian today can't compare to 50 years ago. We may be entering into a period unlike any experienced in Western Christianity before, where we will be persecuted for our faith, where we will actually pay a price for it, where we will not be embraced by culture as we were only a generation ago, and where we will be seen and treated as outsiders and threats.

We must have boldness under the power of the Holy Spirit so we can be witnesses in the middle of this generation. We cannot allow the alternative to happen. We can't remain silent and hidden. We can't afford to hide our light under a basket. Faith is personal, but it is never private. God never meant for us to keep to ourselves what Jesus has done for us and the world. The cross and the resurrection are the best news history has ever recorded, and you and I have been entrusted with that message for our time. Each of us will stand accountable to God for what we have done with the gospel message in our generation. We are not responsible for our parents' generation, nor are we responsible for our grandchildren's generation. We are simply responsible for our own.

> *Faith is personal, but it is never private.*

God calls every believer to be a witness. This job does not belong to pastors and missionaries alone. It's *our* job, and it belongs to all of us. The reason God has positioned us throughout our lives—in school, work, our neighborhoods, and among our friends—is to be salt and light in those places. He has placed us as missionaries to share His message with the people around us. The Holy Spirit wants to partner with us and empower us to reach those in our Jerusalem, Judea, Samaria, and ends of the earth. We need the power of the Holy Spirit to do it well—to be bold, to share our faith, to know the Word, to respond to the needs around us, to have words of knowledge and wisdom in due season, and to pray for others in their times of need.

WE CAN GIVE IMPARTATION

The Holy Spirit imparts through us. Allow me to explain. The apostle Paul writes,

> Now there are varieties of gifts, but the same Spirit; and there are varieties of service, but the same Lord; and there are varieties of activities, but it is the same God who empowers them all in everyone. To each is given the manifestation of the Spirit for the common good (1 Corinthians 12:4–7).

The last verse in this passage tells us we have received the Spirit for "the common good." The Holy Spirit dwells within you not only to seal and sanctify you but also to empower and work through you to bless others—to *impart* what He's given you to others.

When you study the miracles and prophecies (or what I refer to as the *dynamic works of the Holy Spirit*) in the Bible, you will discover that almost 90 percent of them occurred outside of a church setting. Where, then, did they take place? They took place in people's houses, in the marketplace, in front of the synagogue, and in the streets.

Why did the Holy Spirit work in these places? Because He is pursuing those who need to be drawn and convicted, regenerated, sealed, led, guided, and empowered. The Holy Spirit is seeking to save those who are lost. And through whom will He do all of this? Those who are willing to be His carriers—those in whom He dwells and with whom He partners. The Spirit wants to use you and me.

Father, we do not want our faith to be stagnant or secret. We refuse to submit to the pressures of this world. According to Your Word in 2 Corinthians 10:5, we capture our thoughts and command them to obey Christ. Lord, let religious traditions fall to the ground. Let lies and deceptions be dispelled by the glory of Your light and truth.

Lord, let us never be satisfied with "normal." Let us be discontent with average. Stir and fan into flame a hunger for Your gifts and callings in our lives. Holy Spirit, we invite you to come and inhabit us. Have Your way. In Jesus' name, Amen.

STUDY GUIDE

THE HOLY SPIRIT is not some distant entity making things happen for no reason. No, He is an active partner in our lives, providing us intimate access to God the Father. Once you have that access, that means God is near to you. You can receive direct revelation from Him. He will lead you the way He led Jesus in the wilderness. The Holy Spirit intercedes for us when we don't know what to say, and He empowers us so that we can impart that power to others.

REVIEW

1. Why do disciples get access to God the Father through the Holy Spirit? How does He provide us with that same access?
2. Is there any conflict between the Holy Spirit and the Word? How do the Holy Spirit and the Word work together to reveal the nature of God and His love for us?
3. Who else besides the Holy Spirit is interceding for us? What is the main thing the Holy Spirit and Jesus empower us for?

REFLECTION

1. Have you seen the Holy Spirit at work in providing access to God, either for you or other believers? What did that look like?

2. What does it mean to you to pray *with* the Holy Spirit? How can you bring the Spirit more directly into your prayer life?

3. God has empowered and called all of us to be witnesses. How has God called you to be a witness to those around you?

SCHOOL OF THE SPIRIT 201

INTRODUCTION
TO THE BAPTISM
IN THE HOLY SPIRIT

CHAPTER 5

THE PROMISE OF THE FATHER

And while staying with them he ordered them not to depart from Jerusalem, but to wait for the promise of the Father, which, he said, "you heard from me."

—Jesus in Acts 1:4

NOT TOO LONG AGO, we conducted a three-weekend, live Q & A at Radiant Church and addressed some of the hottest topics in our contemporary culture. We titled the series *Red Hot*, using the slogan, "This could get spicy." Our advertisement for the final week of the series said, "It's wildcard weekend, and anything goes!" As lead pastor and facilitator, I was the guy who had to field the questions. And wouldn't you know, the very first question was a stumper! One of the children in our Radiant Kids asked, "Pastor Lee, why did God create the appendix?" *Boom!* I was in over my head already. I sheepishly admitted I had no clue why God gave us an appendix. I replied, "It's kind of like asking why IKEA includes all those extra parts in their packages." That was my best answer.

Most of the following questions were at least on topics where my education and training could help me. I answered questions such as "Can a Christian be demonized?" or "Is there such a thing as a literal hell?" Now you understand why we gave the series the title we did.

Well, the topic I am about to address could easily have been included in that last week of Q & A. Whenever someone brings up the baptism (or infilling) in the Holy Spirit, the conversation tends to get hot. In fact, the baptism in the Holy Spirit is often a lightning rod that draws heated debate.

As I said in the introduction, when we don't have a frame of reference for something, that *something* can seem a bit strange or weird to us. Once we learn more about a given subject, we may find ourselves less uncomfortable with it, or we may even fully embrace it. I hope and pray this change will happen for you as you read about the baptism in the Holy Spirit—or what Jesus called the "promise of the Father" (see Acts 1:4).

THE PROMISE FORETOLD IN THE OLD TESTAMENT

As I explained in the previous section, the Bible teaches us about the significance of the Holy Spirit in the lives of believers. The entire Old Testament pointed toward a time when God would pour out the Holy Spirit upon "all flesh" and not just prophets, priests, judges, kings, or select individuals. God would accomplish this promise through the Messiah and create a nation (the Church) of priests and kings (see Revelation 1:6). The fulfillment of that promise would also be marked by supernatural signs and wonders and the outbreak of the miraculous, which would lead to the full manifestation of the Kingdom of God on the earth.

The entire Old Testament pointed toward a time when God would pour out the Holy Spirit upon "all flesh" and not just prophets, priests, judges, kings, or select individuals.

The Kingdom of God was Jesus' message in His preaching and teaching. He said, "Behold, the kingdom of God is in the midst of you" (Luke 17:21). Jesus came inaugurating the Kingdom of God. It was not the first time, however, that His audience had heard the phrase *the Kingdom of God,* for it was a common concept in their messianic hope—a biblical hope. The prophets of the Old Testament had been declaring not only the Messiah's coming and the restoration of the nation of Israel but also the coming of the Kingdom that would eclipse all other kingdoms.

The prophet Isaiah, for example, predicted a child would be born and His Kingdom would know no end (see Isaiah 9:6–7). The prophet Zechariah spoke about a day when "many nations shall join themselves to the LORD" and become God's people (see Zechariah 2:11). And the prophet Habakkuk declared,

> For the earth will be filled
>   with the knowledge of the glory of the LORD
>   as the waters cover the sea (Habakkuk 2:14).

The concept of the Kingdom of God (His reign and rule over the whole earth) was a messianic promise. When Jesus came proclaiming the Kingdom of God, He wasn't introducing a new idea. He was speaking about Israel's hope and expectation.

Additionally, when the Messiah and His Kingdom came, there would be a shift or change in the relationship between people and God. They would no longer access Him solely through priests, judges, prophets, or other intermediaries. They would now have direct access. Many Old Testament prophecies attest to this change in relationship, but I want to focus on two specific prophecies that directly address the promise of the Holy Spirit from the Father: Ezekiel 36:27 and Joel 2:28–29.

Speaking on the Lord's behalf, Ezekiel prophesied, "I will put my Spirit within you, and cause you to walk in my statutes and be careful to obey my rules" (Ezekiel 36:27). Our experience can attest to the fulfillment of this prophecy. In School of the Spirit 101, we learned that we are born again and regenerated by the Holy Spirit, and He now abides in us. The reason we know this truth is because we're living on the other side of Jesus' death, resurrection, and ascension, as well as the outpouring of the Holy Spirit that inaugurated the era of the Kingdom of God in which we're now living. In the Old Testament, however, the Holy Spirit did not dwell within people. He *came upon* people. For the most part, the Spirit came upon the prophets, enabling them to prophesy and speak on God's behalf to the nation of Israel. He came upon the judges and the kings, such as Deborah and David, so they would be anointed with wisdom, revelation, counsel, might, and courage as they led God's people. The Holy Spirit also came upon the priests as they served in the Temple or the house of the Lord.

The Old Testament does contain a few exceptions. For example, Exodus records this account of Bezalel, a craftsman involved in constructing the Tabernacle:

> See, the LORD has called by name Bezalel the son of Uri, son
> of Hur, of the tribe of Judah; and he has filled him with the
> Spirit of God, with skill, with intelligence, with knowledge,
> and with all craftsmanship.... And he has inspired him to teach
> (Exodus 35:30–31, 34).

Bezalel was filled with the Holy Spirit, which enabled him to
design the Tabernacle. Another example is the prophet Micah.
When confronting the false prophets of Israel, Micah declared
of himself,

> But as for me, I am filled with power,
>   with the Spirit of the LORD,
>   and with justice and might,
> to declare to Jacob his transgression
>   and to Israel his sin (Micah 3:8).

So the Holy Spirit did indwell a few people during the Old
Testament period, but this was not the norm. During that time,
the average person had the Law and leaders like the priests,
prophets, judges, and kings who could tell him what God said. The
people recognized that their leaders possessed a special or unique
relationship with God. They witnessed something different in
those specially anointed men and women, a quality and experience that was different from their own. Therefore, when God
spoke through Ezekiel and said, "I will put my Spirit within you,"
that was a whole new way of thinking—a new paradigm. With the
exception of what Micah proclaimed, even the prophets, judges,
priests, and kings did not have the Holy Spirit abiding *within*
them. They would have the Holy Spirit "come upon" them.
They would be clothed, as it were, in His strength and power

for a specific purpose and a specific time, but the Spirit was not placed permanently inside them. When God put His Spirit upon someone in the Old Testament, He was giving a limited, supernatural empowerment of grace for a singular reason.

The idea that the Holy Spirit would dwell within a person had to be mind-boggling. The people of the Old Testament surely struggled to comprehend that concept. To the Jewish mind of the day, God dwelt in the Temple. He abided in the special room of the Holy of Holies. The people understood that if a priest entered the Holy of Holies and was not cleansed or purified, then he would fall over dead! That was their frame of reference. Consequently, they had an intense fear of the presence of God and had a holy awe and reverence for it. However, God had something else entirely in mind, and He gave Ezekiel the words to tell the people that a day would come when He "will give you a new heart, and a new spirit ... and remove the heart of stone from your flesh and give you a heart of flesh" (Ezekiel 36:26). God would put His Spirit inside His people.

God said this through His prophet Joel:

> And it shall come to pass afterward,
>   that I will pour out my Spirit on all flesh;
> your sons and your daughters shall prophesy,
>   your old men shall dream dreams,
>   and your young men shall see visions.
> Even on the male and female servants
>   in those days I will pour out my Spirit (Joel 2:28–29).

To what time was God pointing when He said, "In those days"? It was the time of the Messiah. God would reconstitute Israel and initiate and inaugurate His plans for the whole earth to come under His lordship and the reign of His Kingdom.

Joel declared the promise of the Father—the outpouring of the Holy Spirit—by using language that meant a saturating or dousing rain. It was as if God was saying, "I'm going to pour it out in such a way that nobody is going to escape dry. I'm not just going to pour it out on David. I'm not just going to pour it out in My Temple. I'm going to pour it out on the whole earth." Notice how the prophecy erased the lines that distinguished people and places from each other. Again, using my own words, it was as if God was saying, "It's going to be young men and old men. It's going to be men and women. It's going to be rich and poor. Everyone is included. There will be no gender differences. No economic distinctions. No age limits. *All* flesh. I'm going to pour out My Spirit on *all* flesh."

There will be no gender differences.
No economic distinctions.
No age limits. All *flesh.*

You see, old men typically don't dream dreams. Young men are the dreamers, but God said His outpouring of the Holy Spirit was going to be so powerful that it was going to rejuvenate old men so they would dream like young men. It was going to activate and do something even in servants. Gender lines, age limitations, and all the other distinctions we make in our religious mindsets, in which we say, "These are the type of people who do this. These are the type of people who do that," are gone. God said He was going to crush our old paradigms. His promise of empowerment through the Person of His Holy Spirit was going to come upon "all flesh."

THE GOSPELS AND THE PROMISE OF THE FATHER

More prophets arose after Joel. They continued to point the people toward the coming of the Messiah. Malachi was one of those prophets. Between Malachi and the beginning of the Gospels in the New Testament, no additional books of the Bible were written. Silence fell over God's people for more than 400 years. Consider what the people must have been thinking and wondering. When would the Messiah come? When would the prophecies of Ezekiel and Joel be fulfilled? When would the Kingdom and rule of God come?

Then John the Baptist entered the scene. He arrived as a forerunner, preparing the way for the coming of the Promised One. This is how the apostle Matthew recorded John's words:

> I baptize you with water for repentance, but he who is coming after me is mightier than I, whose sandals I am not worthy to carry. He will baptize you with the Holy Spirit and fire (Matthew 3:11).

Here is the account in the gospels of Mark and Luke:

> After me comes he who is mightier than I, the strap of whose sandals I am not worthy to stoop down and untie. I have

baptized you with water, but he will baptize you with the Holy Spirit (Mark 1:7–8).

I baptize you with water, but he who is mightier than I is coming, the strap of whose sandals I am not worthy to untie. He will baptize you with the Holy Spirit and fire (Luke 3:16).

Each of the three writers of the Synoptic Gospels[1] gave very similar accounts of John the Baptist's words. How, then, did the apostle John record John the Baptist's words?

I baptize with water, but among you stands one you do not know, even he who comes after me, the strap of whose sandal I am not worthy to untie.... I myself did not know him, but he who sent me to baptize with water said to me, "He on whom you see the Spirit descend and remain, this is he who baptizes with the Holy Spirit." And I have seen and have borne witness that this is the Son of God (John 1:26–27, 33–34).

John the Baptist announced the arrival of the Kingdom of God and called people to repentance so they would be ready for the Son of God, whom he had seen.

Interestingly, all four of the Gospels contain the same statement from John the Baptist, with only minor wording differences. The fact that it occurs in all four Gospels is quite noteworthy because few things are recorded in all four accounts. Many of the same parables, miracles, and events are recorded in the Synoptic Gospels (Matthew, Mark, and Luke). These Gospels share much of the same source material and the same stories, especially Matthew and Mark. If you are reading the New Testament for the first time, then you might read the first three Gospels and get a bit of a shock when you arrive at John's Gospel. You'll soon realize that John took a whole new spin on the events of Jesus' life. John's style of writing is different, and he shared different miracles. It's not as if John differed with the others' views about Jesus. He simply filled in some of the gaps as he wrote from his unique perspective. Even so, the fact is significant that John the Baptist's statement regarding Jesus' being the Baptizer with the Holy Spirit is in all four Gospels. This fact should confirm to us that the baptism in the Holy Spirit is a significant New Testament doctrine, and it was also important to Jesus.

> *John the Baptist's statement regarding Jesus' being the Baptizer with the Holy Spirit is in all four Gospels.*

Different people depict Jesus in many different ways, but John the Baptist described Jesus' ministry and said He would be the One who would baptize people with the Holy Spirit. The word *baptism* is derived from the Greek word *baptizo,* and it means to submerge, to overwhelm, to saturate, and to take something under the water. In fact, *baptism* is actually an English borrow word from Greek, because when the Bible was being translated, no English equivalent existed for the act of baptism other than *submerge.* Therefore, if you get baptized in water, then you go under the water. This practice was not difficult for Jewish people to understand; they were accustomed to washing their bodies for ceremonial purification. In the Hebrew, the term for this practice is *mikveh.* In this ritual, the entire body was immersed for cleansing. It was a baptism. John the Baptist was doing a kind of *mikveh*. He was calling people to repentance and then baptizing them—not in the still and sometimes stagnant waters of a cistern but in the living, moving water of the Jordan River.

In a sense, John the Baptist was saying, "I'm baptizing you with water so that when you see the Messiah, you'll understand what He's going to do for you by the Holy Spirit. I want you to picture a rushing river of living water coming from the Spirit. It will overwhelm, saturate, and submerge you in the power and the Person of the Holy Spirit. That's what the Baptizer is going to do."

JESUS AND THE PROMISE OF THE FATHER

As I have discussed, the promise of the Father was prophesied in the Old Testament, proclaimed by John the Baptist, and included in all four Gospels. But what did Jesus have to say about it? He referenced the promise of the Father or the baptism in the Holy Spirit as a gift He would personally offer His followers after His death, burial, resurrection, and glorification. What's more, Jesus encouraged those followers to go to Jerusalem to wait for the outpouring of the Holy Spirit before attempting to fulfill any part of the Great Commission He had given to them.

Jesus said,

> Thus it is written, that the Christ should suffer and on the third day rise from the dead, and that repentance for the forgive-

ness of sins should be proclaimed in his name to all nations, beginning from Jerusalem. You are witnesses of these things (Luke 24:46–48).

Jesus spoke these words to His disciples after His resurrection. At the time, He was in the middle of talking to them about their doubts and giving them an opportunity to touch Him so they could prove to themselves He was alive, real, and had come back to them. After telling them what they would be proclaiming about Him in all the nations, Jesus ate some broiled fish. Then Jesus concluded His conversation with this: "Behold, I am sending the promise of my Father upon you. But stay in the city until you are clothed with power from on high" (Luke 24:49). Jesus was telling His disciples that He was about to fulfill the promise of the Father, which is what the Old Testament prophets had foretold and what John the Baptist had announced. Jesus told His disciples to stay in Jerusalem and wait.

When the Spirit came upon select people in the Old Testament, it was as if God put a garment upon them. In another translation of Luke 24:49, Jesus says, "Behold, I send the Promise of My Father upon you; but tarry in the city of Jerusalem until you are endued with power from on high" (NKJV). Jesus was telling them to wait in the city until they were clothed with power. He said the power would come "from on high," which means it would come from the celestial, not the terrestrial. It was as if Jesus was saying, "I'm going to the Father, but all of you hold on and wait right here. I'm going to make some heavenly connections for you."

Notice a few verses later that Luke 24 closes with Jesus' ascension, and the narrative seems to end. But if you turn to

Acts 1, then you'll find that Luke picks up where he left off: "the day [Jesus] was taken up" (Acts 1:2). Luke informs his readers that after Jesus rose from the dead, He appeared to the disciples several times over the course of 40 days, presenting "himself alive to them after his suffering by many proofs ... and speaking about the kingdom of God" (Acts 1:3). Later, in the apostle Paul's account, we learn that Jesus appeared to "more than five hundred brothers at one time" (1 Corinthians 15:6). When we put all the accounts together, we confirm that Jesus walked in a glorified, resurrected body, meeting with His disciples for 40 days and teaching them about things pertaining to the Kingdom of God.

In the last few days Jesus had with His disciples before He ascended into heaven, He gave these instructions:

> He ordered them not to depart from Jerusalem, but to wait for the promise of the Father, which, he said, "you heard from me; for John baptized with water, but you will be baptized with the Holy Spirit not many days from now" (Acts 1:4–5).

Jesus directly connected the promise of the Father with the baptism with the Holy Spirit. Here's the mathematical equation: *The promise of the Father equals the baptism in the Holy Spirit.* I've already written about this connection, but I want you to see how Jesus said the two were one and the same thing.

The promise of the Father equals the baptism in the Holy Spirit.

In John's gospel, the writer covers Jesus' resurrection and appearances to Peter and Mary Magdalene. Then in the closing chapter, John shares a jaw-dropping scene as Jesus appears to His disciples. They were gathered together in lockdown in the upper room "for fear of the Jews" (John 20:19). The doors were locked, and suddenly "Jesus came and stood among them." He just appeared! One moment He was outside the upper room, on the other side of the locked doors, and then Jesus stood inside with the disciples. Verse 20 says, "He showed them His hands and his side," giving them the proofs of His resurrection that Luke wrote about. Then Jesus said,

> "Peace be with you. As the Father has sent me, even so I am sending you." And when he had said this, he breathed on them and said to them, "Receive the Holy Spirit" (John 20:21–22).

What is happening in these verses? Let's go back to Genesis 2 and recall the scene in the Garden of Eden when God created Adam. Verse 7 says God "breathed into his nostrils the breath of life, and the man became a living creature." The Lord breathed His spirit into Adam. Remember, the words *spirit, wind,* and *breath* come from the same Hebrew term. Now, return to John 20. Jesus breathed on His disciples and said, "Receive the Holy Spirit" (v. 22). Receive the *wind*. Receive the *breath*. Receive the *life*. What exactly took place in that upper room? I believe that was the moment when the disciples were born again. Prior to Jesus' death on the cross, they were not born again because Jesus had not yet paid for the sins of humanity. Ezekiel said God's goal was for the Spirit to dwell within us, but Jesus had to deal with sin first. Only He could make us righteous before God, and only then could God dwell within us by the Holy Spirit.

Forty days later, in Acts 1, Jesus told the disciples to wait in Jerusalem for the promise of the Father or the baptism with the Holy Spirit. They have received the Spirit in conversion and regeneration a few weeks before and were saved, but there was something distinct that had not yet happened to them. I am referring to the Holy Spirit coming upon them with power so they could serve God and fulfill His purposes. The disciples needed the anointing of the Holy Spirit to be placed upon them before they could attempt to fulfill the Great Commission. Of course, the Holy Spirit was already in them from the standpoint that they were saved, sealed, and in the process of being sanctified. He was illuminating and walking with them, which means positionally He dwelled in them.

According to Luke, Jesus was essentially telling His disciples, "I don't want you to leave the city of Jerusalem until something else happens—something that hasn't come yet. It's different. The same Holy Spirit you received upon your salvation will now come upon you with power so you can be My witnesses in Jerusalem, Judea, Samaria, and to the ends of the earth." They will be endued, clothed, or baptized in the Holy Spirit. Jesus said they would receive power from on high. The Greek word translated here as *power* is *dunamis*. The English words *dynamic* and *dynamite* are derived from it. It connotes something that is explosive, and from a theological perspective, it is the supernaturally-sourced power of God.

Here is the unveiling of the promise the Father had given throughout biblical history. The Lord had spoken through His prophets about the day when the Spirit would indwell us. Like every priest, judge, prophet, and king who had the Holy Spirit come upon them for service and the purposes of God in the Old

Testament, the followers of Jesus were now in the Kingdom of God as His prophets, priests, and kings. They would have the same Spirit come upon them in baptism. They would have something distinct and something more from the Spirit's indwelling them upon their salvation. They would need to receive the Holy Spirit put upon them with supernatural power that would give them the ability to live supernatural lives and fulfill their supernatural ministry in a way beyond their own strength.

You may be wondering, *Well, if the Holy Spirit is within me when I am saved, then why do I need Him also to be upon me?* When we talk about God being upon us, it's a different dynamic in both quality and type. It is true that God always dwells within us. Every believer has the Holy Spirit. You don't receive 90 percent of the Holy Spirit upon salvation and then the missing 10 percent upon the baptism or infilling in the Spirit. No, it's not like that. Just as the disciples did in John 20, you get the whole Holy Spirit with your regeneration. What I'm writing about is a completely different dynamic, a different reality, in which the Holy Spirit comes *upon* you. It's like God putting His hand on you and plugging you into a super-charger that gives you access to the supernatural realm and the power of heaven. It's the promise of the Father. Jesus defined it as the baptism in the Holy Spirit, and He understood His followers would need the same power from on high that He had so they could fulfill the Great Commission. And so do you, and so do I. Just to prove it, we will look in the next chapter at how the baptism in the Spirit affected the first-century disciples as recorded in the book of Acts.

> *It's like God putting His hand on you and plugging you into a super-charger that gives you access to the supernatural realm and the power of heaven.*

Father, we come before You with hearts filled with gratitude and thanksgiving. We are thankful You have revealed Yourself to us and pursued us. Thank You for giving us the gift of Your Holy Spirit upon our salvation. As we focus on the gift of the Holy Spirit, give us heavenly eyes, Kingdom ears, and submitted hearts. Make us receptive and hungry for everything You have for us. We thank You that Your Word is a light unto our path and a lamp unto our feet. We declare that no voice besides the Holy Spirit's will have access to our hearts today. We welcome You to come, Holy Spirit. Speak to us. Illuminate your Word for us and strengthen and empower us. In Jesus' name, Amen.

CHAPTER 5

STUDY GUIDE

THE BAPTISM IN THE HOLY SPIRIT can be a lightning rod that draws heated debate. However, the indwelling of the Holy Spirit is a promise of God the Father to which the entire Old Testament pointed. Many of the prophets spoke of it, but Joel's prophecy is the most direct, relating to the future indwelling in the Kingdom. John the Baptist declared that Jesus would be the one to baptize people in the Holy Spirit. Jesus told His disciples they would receive this promise, and it was fulfilled at Pentecost. God is now not only *in* His people but also *upon* His people.

REVIEW

1. Why is the baptism in the Holy Spirit often a controversial topic?
2. Who were some of the Old Testament prophets that pointed to the future indwelling of the Spirit? Did the Spirit indwell anyone during the Old Testament era?
3. What does the word *baptism* mean? What is the difference between receiving the Holy Spirit inside you when you are saved and having the Holy Spirit come upon you with the baptism in the Spirit?

REFLECTION

1. Has the issue of the baptism in the Holy Spirit been difficult for you or someone you know to come to grips with? Why is that the case?
2. How is John's depiction of Jesus' life different from that of the other Gospel writers? Read John chapters 1 and 20 with the eternal promise of the Father in mind.
3. Think about when Jesus manifested Himself in the upper room on Pentecost. How do you think the disciples felt? How would you have felt when Jesus said, "Receive the Holy Spirit"?

THE OUTPOURING
OF THE HOLY SPIRIT

*Now many signs and wonders were regularly done among the
people by the hands of the apostles.... And more than ever believers
were added to the Lord, multitudes of both men and women.*

—Acts 5:12, 14

I TRY TO READ through the book of Acts at least a few times a
year because it stirs my faith for the Church. It's a powerful,
wild ride! It shows the impact God wants us to have on the
world and who He calls us to be—the Spirit-empowered Church
propelled forward in the power of the Holy Spirit with signs
and wonders following.

After Jesus ascended to heaven, His disciples were infused
with power from on high. Remember, these were the same
followers who had scattered like ants from the Garden of
Gethsemane on the night Jesus was betrayed and arrested.
Their new empowerment changed everything. In the first
century, those Spirit-empowered messengers carried the seed
of the gospel to Italy, Greece, Spain, Egypt, India, Ethiopia, and
too many other places to list here. In other words, they went
to the ends of the earth. They became *apostles,* which means
"ones who are sent." That is the reason why Jesus had told
them to wait in Jerusalem for the promise of the Father. There

was no way they could fulfill the Great Commission without it. They needed the power of the Holy Spirit to endure beatings and other kinds of persecutions and to face death because of their witness.

In the second chapter of this book, we learned that the Holy Spirit enabled the apostles and other followers of Jesus to face the persecutions of Rome. In this chapter, we will take a closer look at the account of the outpouring of the Holy Spirit on the Day of Pentecost in Acts 2.

THE ASCENSION

In Acts 1:1–4, Luke sets the stage for the ascension of Jesus into heaven. The writer explains how Jesus instructed His followers to wait in Jerusalem for the promise of the Father. Then he recounts the conversation Jesus had with the disciples as they were gathered there on the Mount of Olives. Finally, Luke shares Jesus' last words to the disciples: "You will receive power when the Holy Spirit has come upon you, and you will be my witnesses ... to the end of the earth" (Acts 1:8).

What happened next? Jesus began to rise in the air as the disciples watched. Did you catch that? Jesus came up off *terra firma* and, using Luke's words, "a cloud took him out of their sight" (v. 9). Imagine, for a moment, that you're one of Jesus' followers gathered there. One second, you're talking to Jesus, listening to Him field a question about when He is going to restore your nation, your people, and—*snap!*—He's gone. Where did He go? He is the same person who died on a cross and rose from death three days later. This is the Man who had been outside the locked doors of the upper room when—*boom!*—you see Him standing in the room. So what do you do now? You keep staring in the direction where you last saw Him. And as you look up into the sky, trying to find a trace of Him—*behold!*—two men appear out of nowhere and ask you why you're looking up into the sky.

Your mind is running full speed to catch up with what is happening, and you think to yourself, *Okay, Jesus just flew away, and now these two men in white robes have appeared out of nowhere and asked me what I'm looking at?* Then they tell you, "This Jesus, who was taken up from you into heaven, will come in the same way as you saw him go into heaven" (Acts 1:11).

Now step out of your imagination and let me to take you into mine for a moment. I must admit I am blown away when I read the next line in Luke's account: "Then they returned to Jerusalem from the mount called Olivet" (v. 12). Wait a minute, Luke! Where's the rest of the story? What conversations did the disciples have? Did they simply take the word of these two white-robed men?

Luke doesn't give us the answers to those questions. Nevertheless, he succeeds at getting our attention. He aptly sets the stage for the events that will follow in the rest of the book of Acts—namely, the dynamic, supernatural partnership of the Holy Spirit with the men and women who will be the first ones to be called Christians.

Luke tells his readers that about 120 people gathered in the upper room, including the disciples and Jesus' mothers and brothers. "All these with one accord were devoting themselves to prayer" (Acts 1:14), which means they all agreed that the most important thing they could do at that moment was pray. There was also an important matter they needed to attend to: selecting a replacement for Judas. Verse 26 says, "The lot fell on Matthias" (Acts 1:26).

ON THE DAY OF PENTECOST

Luke opens the second chapter of Acts by telling his readers that it is the day of Pentecost. For about 10 days, 120 of Jesus' followers have been gathered in Jerusalem in the upper room. It's been a long, 10-day prayer meeting. At that point, they still expected something, but they had no idea what it was. The only thing they knew for sure was that Jesus told them to go to Jerusalem and wait. There was no calendar that marked the exact day or hour when the promise of the Father would arrive. And God made them wait. For 10 days, He made them wait. The number 10 has significance in the Bible because it represents testing and completion.

Let's let Luke take the story from here:

> When the day of Pentecost arrived, they were all together in one place. And suddenly there came from heaven a sound like a mighty rushing wind, and it filled the entire house where they were sitting. And divided tongues as of fire appeared to them and rested on each one of them. And they were all filled with the Holy Spirit and began to speak in other tongues as the Spirit gave them utterance.
>
> Now there were dwelling in Jerusalem Jews, devout men from every nation under heaven. And at this sound the multitude came together, and they were bewildered, because

each one was hearing them speak in his own language. And they were amazed and astonished, saying, "Are not all these who are speaking Galileans? And how is it that we hear, each of us in his own native language? Parthians and Medes and Elamites and residents of Mesopotamia, Judea and Cappadocia, Pontus and Asia, Phrygia and Pamphylia, Egypt and the parts of Libya belonging to Cyrene, and visitors from Rome, both Jews and proselytes, Cretans and Arabians—we hear them telling in our own tongues the mighty works of God." And all were amazed and perplexed, saying to one another, "What does this mean?" But others mocking said, "They are filled with new wine."

But Peter, standing with the eleven, lifted up his voice and addressed them: "Men of Judea and all who dwell in Jerusalem, let this be known to you, and give ear to my words. For these people are not drunk, as you suppose, since it is only the third hour of the day. But this is what was uttered through the prophet Joel:

'And in the last days it shall be, God declares,
that I will pour out My Spirit on all flesh'" (Acts 2:17).

Remember, in Acts 1:4–5, Jesus had told His followers "to wait for the promise of the Father," saying they would "be baptized with the Holy Spirit not many days from now." Jesus linked the promise of the Father with the baptism with the Holy Spirit. And Peter's sermon in Acts 2, which came as a response to the questions from those who wanted to know what was happening, made the connection back to Joel 2. This is what God had promised through the prophet in the Old Testament, and it was being fulfilled right then and there through Jesus. Peter recited a good portion of Joel 2 to those gathered around, and the message was clear: *This is that! And then is now!*

Don't miss the significance of the day on which the Holy Spirit fell on the Church. In Acts 2:1, Luke notes that these happenings were on the day of Pentecost. Jews from all over the world would have made a pilgrimage to Jerusalem to celebrate on that day. Pentecost was one of Israel's high holy days, and many Jews came to observe it with a feast. *Pentecost* is derived from a Greek word meaning 'fifty days,' and as such, it occurred fifty days after Passover. Pentecost commemorated an important event that took place much earlier in Israel's history, during the time of Moses. It signified the day he received of the Law from God at Mount Sinai:

> On the morning of the third day there were thunders and lightnings and a thick cloud on the mountain and a very loud trumpet blast, so that all the people in the camp trembled. Then Moses brought the people out of the camp to meet God, and they took their stand at the foot of the mountain. Now Mount Sinai was wrapped in smoke because the LORD descended on it in fire. The smoke of it went up like the smoke of a kiln, and the whole mountain trembled greatly. And as the sound of the trumpet grew louder and louder, Moses spoke, and God answered him in thunder. The LORD came down on Mount Sinai, to the top of the mountain. And the LORD called Moses to the top of the mountain, and Moses went up (Exodus 19:16–20).

If you follow the remainder of the Sinai account, you will read that Moses came back down, and God spoke the Law over the people of Israel (see Exodus 19:21–20:17). After the last commandment was spoken, the text says, "Now when all the people saw the thunder and the flashes of lightning and the sound of the trumpet and the mountain smoking, the people were afraid and trembled, and they stood far off" (Exodus 20:18). Imagine what it must have been like for them. These were the same people who had been slaves but were miraculously delivered by God from Egyptian rule. They had heard all the stories of Abraham, Isaac, and Jacob, yet all they had known in their experience was slavery and subjugation. They had witnessed God do some incredible miracles to bring them out of bondage. For example, the parting of the Red Sea was an amazing, supernatural feat! Then, there they were at Mount Sinai, and God came down in a supernatural thunderstorm. The Lord's voice came with lightning and resounded like thunder, and smoke billowed all about the mountain. They heard heavenly trumpets sounding around them. There they were, gathered at the base of Mount Sinai, and all this happened as God came down on the mountain to speak. It was a phenomenal scene.

Rabbinic tradition contains some interesting commentary about this event. The day is known as *Shavuot*, and it is regarded in Jewish culture as the wedding day of Yahweh to His people, Israel. It was as if the Lord came running to His beloved people at the place of their meeting, much like a bridegroom eagerly rushes to receive his bride. Having rescued her from Pharaoh's brutality, the Lord came to His bride with passion and fury. Accordingly, the Law served as the *Ketubah*—the marriage contract—between the Lord and Israel.[1]

Looking once again at the biblical scene in Exodus, the children of Israel then asked Moses to speak to them instead of God continuing to speak. They were so terrified that they thought they would die if they had to endure more of God's direct speech (see Exodus 20:19). See, God's intention was not that Israel would be good law keepers. His intention was always for Israel to be a nation of kings and priests—a holy bride married to Him. The Lord wanted to have a living relationship with Israel (and subsequently with us). He wanted a partnership in which He would speak to His bride and engage with her both supernaturally and literally. The Lord wanted to write the Law on her heart because she had encountered Him (see Jeremiah 31:33). Sadly, Israel settled for tablets of stone, and so have many of us as believers.

Additionally, rabbinic tradition says,

> On the occasion of [the giving] of the Torah, the [children of Israel] not only heard the Lord's Voice, but actually saw the sound waves as they emerged from the Lord's mouth. They visualized them as a fiery substance. Each commandment that left the Lord's mouth traveled around the entire camp and then came back to every Jew individually.[2]

Can you see the similarity between the "fiery substance" upon the heads of those gathered at Sinai and those waiting in the upper room?

But that's not all! Rabbinic tradition says when God spoke the Law, He spoke it in 70 different languages simultaneously.[3] It is believed that there were 70 ethnic or language groups on the earth at the time the Lord gave the Law and that there was a mixed multitude along with the Jewish people at Sinai. So when God spoke His laws, they were delivered in the known languages of every nationality on earth so that every nation could have a relationship with Him. His desire was never to have only one nation. Israel was to be the light to *all* nations. When the other nations of the earth saw the goodness of God and the uniqueness of the people of God—their *shalom* or perfect peace—then they would be provoked and want the relationship with God that Israel had. God wanted to make the other nations jealous by how He blessed Israel. But remember the response of those gathered around Mount Sinai: they were afraid they were going to die from encountering God in the thunder, lightning, and trumpet blasts. So the people chose to hear from an intermediary instead. They chose to let God encounter Moses, and then Moses could tell them what they needed to know. Under Moses, God gave the Law, but under Jesus, God gave the Spirit.

His desire was never to have only one nation. Israel was to be the light to all nations.

For hundreds of years, Israel commemorated Pentecost. Shortly after Jesus' resurrection, Jews from every part of the Roman Empire came to Jerusalem to celebrate Pentecost, which they also knew as the Feast of Harvest. Then, after Peter's sermon, 3,000 new people believed in the Good News about Jesus. They were saved. Three thousand souls is a harvest!

God doesn't do anything by accident. Jesus gave the disciples specific instructions to follow to prepare them to be baptized in the Holy Spirit. They followed His directions after His ascension, and in God's timing, He poured out the Holy Spirit, which fulfilled Joel's prophecy. And God's timing was for this to happen on the day of Pentecost, when "devout men from every nation under heaven" (Acts 2:5) gathered to commemorate the time when God gave the Law to Moses. God was fulfilling the promises He had inaugurated at Mount Sinai and was now completing in Jesus.

Now, I want to tell you a few more things that happened at Pentecost. Luke says that they were *all* filled with the Holy Spirit. Next, he says, "[They] began to speak in other tongues as the Spirit gave them utterance" (Acts 2:4). The word translated here as *tongues* is simply another word for *languages* or, more specifically, *unknown languages*. In other words, all of the 120 people in the upper room were filled with the Holy Spirit and began to speak in languages unknown to them. None of these were languages that they themselves understood or had learned to speak. It's no wonder the devout men came to see what was happening. They were at a loss to understand how "these Galileans" were speaking foreign languages. Looking back at Acts 2:9–11, consider the possible number of languages spoken by Jesus' 120 followers. There were probably 50 to 70 or more distinct languages being spoken.

Over the years, I have given a lot of study to Acts 2. What I have noticed about the biblical text is that each of the listeners was actually hearing all of the different languages spoken at once, yet they were able to hear what was being said in each person's known language. If we tried to replicate this event today, we could easily gather 120 people who could each speak in a different language. One person might speak French, another Spanish, another Greek, another Arabic, another Hebrew, and so on. If we told them to speak simultaneously, what would we hear? We would likely hear a roar of noise. Granted, our ears would individually tune in to our mother tongues; however, the sound as a whole would likely be confused babbling. What I am telling you is the promise of the Father—the baptism with the Holy Spirit—was supernatural and miraculous. Just as miraculous was that all of the 3,000-plus people heard about the mighty works of God in their own languages. It had to be an act of God, and only God. Yes, they all spoke in tongues. But another way to say this is that those who received the promise of the Father spoke in a *spiritual utterance* or language. I think saying it this way can help douse some of the flames that are kindled when we discuss speaking in tongues.

All 120 followers of Jesus who gathered in the upper room experienced the same spiritual phenomenon; they spoke with spiritual utterance. To the more than 3,000 people who witnessed the event, these believers appeared to be drunk. The onlookers tried to make sense of the sounds they were hearing because they wanted to know was happening. To these witnesses, it sounded like a real ruckus, a great commotion. No matter what it may have sounded like or appeared to be at the beginning, though, the immediate fruit of this infilling of the Holy Spirit was Peter's boldness to preach. There was immediate fruit of evangelism, because 3,000 people were saved that day.

What happened throughout the rest of the book of Acts? It was exactly what Jesus told His followers was going to happen—they were given power from on high. The believers were supernaturally endued with unearthly power, spiritual dynamite, and divine anointing. Similar to Samson's incredible strength, David's power as king, Moses' ability to perform miracles, and the many other people in the Old Testament upon whom the Holy Spirit came, these New Testament believers received a special anointing of the Holy Spirit that supercharged them. This power gave them not only the ability to speak but also the ability to work miracles and signs and wonders. All the believers experienced this, and the fruit of it was not division. The fruit of it was not isolation. The fruit of it was power, evangelism, and signs and wonders.

In the book of Acts, the Church is equipped by God to fulfill the Great Commission in its day. God didn't fill the Temple with His glory, as He did during the time of Solomon, where the priest could not even stand up and minister unto the Lord (see 2 Chronicles 5:14). Rather, the Lord was filling His Temple, the newly-born Church made up of living stones. As we continue to follow Luke's account, we find God kept filling them with His dynamic presence and power. Baptized with the Holy Spirit, the believers went from being fearful and weak to courageous and fruitful.

Baptized with the Holy Spirit, the believers went from being fearful and weak to courageous and fruitful.

Father, thank You for sending Your promise to those early believers. Thank You for enduing them with power. Thank You for sending those first Spirit-empowered messengers and growing Your Church throughout the world. We want to be led in that way by Your Spirit. Change us, equip us, strengthen us, and empower us to carry Your message to the world in our day. Make us bold for Your glory and honor. In Jesus' name, Amen.

STUDY GUIDE

IN ACTS 1, Luke recounts how Jesus' followers waited in Jerusalem to receive the promised power of the Holy Spirit. Ten days later on the day of Pentecost, they received that power. It manifested with miraculous signs, including the ability to speak in foreign languages they did not know. Onlookers could miraculously hear and understand their own languages being spoken, and 3,000 people were saved after hearing Peter's sermon that day. The power believers received through the baptism with the Holy Spirit enabled the growth of the early Church.

REVIEW

1. What is the significance of the number 10 in the Bible? How does this relate to the prophecy in Joel 2?
2. How do the events of the giving of the law at Mt. Sinai and the events in the upper room relate to each other? What do they have in common?
3. How did the events in Acts 1–2 set the stage for the growth of the Church?

REFLECTION

1. What does it mean for you as a Christian to be in a supernatural partnership with the Holy Spirit?

2. Are you able to speak any foreign languages? How many people do you know who can speak more than a second language?
3. How can you imitate the fruit of the Holy Spirit that was released at Pentecost?

THE ACTS PATTERN AND THE OVERFLOW

And these signs will accompany those who believe: in my name they will cast out demons; they will speak in new tongues; they will pick up serpents with their hands; and if they drink any deadly poison, it will not hurt them; they will lay their hands on the sick, and they will recover.

—Jesus in Mark 16:17–18

WEARING MY YARMULKE, I leaned against Jerusalem's Wailing Wall (also known as the Western Wall) and held my Bible opened to Romans 11. I had come to this place on the last day of my trip, my heart burdened for my grandfather. My intent was to pray for him at this most sacred site of the Jewish people. As I had moved toward the Wall, however, I was stirred about the Father's heart for Israel. I silently read that chapter out of Paul's letter to the Romans, and I felt the urge to ask God to save His people. Though my heart was greatly moved and my prayer focused, I reflexively opened my eyes, taking in a vast array of people.

Out of the corner of my eye, I spotted an Orthodox Jewish man moving my direction. He stopped at the Wall about five feet away from me. As I prayed with a burden for Israel to be saved, I noticed this man's big beard covering his face, his long hair, his black wide-brimmed hat, and his phylacteries (small leather boxes containing a few verses of the Scriptures in Hebrew). A prayer shawl draped over his shoulders, and he held a leather-bound Torah. He began to pray.

After some time, I slipped deeper into prayer, which typically means I begin to pray in a spiritual language. I prayed in the Spirit as the apostle Paul encouraged the believers at Corinth and Rome to do. I prayed in what sounded to me like my typical spiritual language, meaning the way I usually do as I pray in the Spirit. Soon, though, I felt a shift in how I was praying. I noticed a sound or a language flowing from my lips that was new. I had, of course, heard people speaking Hebrew at various times during my 10-day stay in Israel, and as I listened to myself pray at the Wall, I began thinking that what was coming out of my mouth sounded a lot like Hebrew. I continued praying this way and even leaned into it because I figured the Spirit was working in this way since I was praying for the people of Israel.

Closing my eyes, I prayed aloud with spiritual utterance while my heart was believing for God to save His people. I never considered someone else might be listening. I figured my voice would simply blend in with the other voices at the Wall. I was totally immersed in prayer when I suddenly felt a hand on my arm. I immediately stopped praying, opened my eyes, and recognized the Orthodox man who had been standing next to me. His hand still rested on my arm when he asked,

"Where are you from?"

"M-M-Michigan," I replied, a bit startled by the encounter.

Then he spun on his heels and walked away, leaving me standing alone again. I couldn't quite figure out what had happened.

As I was trying to piece it all together, one of my fellow travelers named Caleb Culver approached me and blurted out,

"Lee, that was so wild. I heard—"
"Caleb, you won't believe what just happened to me. It was wild—"
"Lee, I didn't know—"
We kept excitedly talking over each other until I finally yielded and let him complete his thought. Caleb said,
"I heard you praying, and I was shocked. I thought what you said sounded like a Hebrew prayer, and I figured you memorized one or something. It was so wild!"

At that moment, Caleb and I recognized something had taken place. It was something only the Holy Spirit could have done.

The memory of that experience has stayed with me. Only God knows what fruit it will bear. Nevertheless, I am certain something happened in that Orthodox man's life. I also know something happened in and Caleb's and my lives as we stood in wonder at what the Holy Spirit accomplished in a brief moment that day. That's the power of the Holy Spirit who wants to work in and through us. He's wild and untamed. The Spirit will not be contained. And He wasn't contained within the Acts of the Apostles either.

The Spirit will not be contained.

As I wrote in the introduction, Jesus is the pattern or prototype for all believers. He is the One who shows us what our relationship with the Holy Spirit should look like. In the book of Acts, another pattern begins to emerge, one that is demonstrated to us in the activity of the apostles as they continued to spread the gospel. The book of Acts contains several accounts of people who received the baptism in the Holy Spirit.

THE SAMARITANS

Luke gives the following account in Acts 8:

> Now when the apostles at Jerusalem heard that Samaria had received the word of God, they sent to them Peter and John, who came down and prayed for them that they might receive the Holy Spirit, for he had not yet fallen on any of them, but they had only been baptized in the name of the Lord Jesus. Then they laid their hands on them and they received the Holy Spirit (Acts 8:14–17).

You may have heard that the Samaritans and Jews tried to avoid each other. That's what made Jesus' parable about the good Samaritan so shocking to those who first heard it. The Samaritans were kind of Jewish but, then again, not. They were considered "half breeds." The Samaritans had their own interpretation of the Torah, along with how they should observe the Law. The Jewish people of Jesus' day considered the Samaritans to be unclean.

When the apostles back in Jerusalem heard that the Samaritans embraced the Good News about Jesus and were saved, Peter and John were sent to pray for them to receive the baptism in the Holy Spirit. I want to pause here for just a moment. You should know thus far that the Samaritans were saved. They were baptized in water in the name of Jesus. At this point, even theologically-minded people in the body of Christ today would say, "Well, the Samaritans were saved and baptized in Jesus' name, and that was it. Now they are believers with us!" Yes, they were saved, but notice that the apostles must have thought the Samaritans needed something else, and it would be good for them to have it. Otherwise, Peter and John would not have been sent to pray for them. The apostles wanted the Samaritans to receive the promise of the Father, just as they had received it.

Let's pick back up with the story. What happened next? Peter and John laid their hands on the Samaritans, and the Samaritans received the Holy Spirit. Now, there's a story within a story here. Apparently, someone named Simon witnessed what happened when the Samaritans received the baptism in the Holy Spirit. Simon was a well-known sorcerer. After what he had seen, he wanted to be able to do what Peter and John did. So Simon said, "Give me this power also, so that anyone on whom I lay my hands may receive the Holy Spirit" (Acts 8:19).

We know from Simon's background that he would have been well-versed in magic, sorcery, incantations, and the like. When he saw the apostles do something he couldn't do, it caught his attention. Something significant must have transpired when Peter and John laid hands on the Samaritans to receive the Holy Spirit. Luke doesn't provide any additional description of what exactly happened when the Samaritans received this baptism, but we do know that Simon wanted the power to do what the apostles did. Furthermore, he was willing to pay for it.

This was no self-help course that Simon could order online. He couldn't buy a starter kit. Peter rebuked him, telling him to repent, and Simon said, "Pray for me to the Lord" (Acts 8:24). However, remember that Simon did witness something that grabbed his attention.

THE ROMANS

In Acts 10, Luke introduces us to a man named Cornelius who lived in Caesarea. He was a Roman centurion, which means he was a Gentile (a non-Jew). Nevertheless, Cornelius believed in the God of the Jews and was generous in giving alms to the poor. He was a man of prayer, and one day while he was praying, he had a vision of an angel sent from God. The angel said to him, "Your prayers and your alms have ascended as a memorial before God. And now send men to Joppa and bring one Simon who is called Peter. He is lodging with one Simon, a tanner, whose house is by the sea" (Acts 10:4–6).

Cornelius obeyed what God told him in the vision and sent messengers to get Peter. Now, Peter would not normally have accepted an invitation to the home of a Gentile, mainly because Jews considered Gentiles and their homes to be unclean. However, while the messengers were on their way, Peter was on a rooftop praying, and God visited him with a supernatural vision. The Lord showed Peter a huge sheet coming out of the sky with many kinds of animals on it (Acts 10:11–13). Then a voice told Peter to get up, kill the animals, and eat them. This command presented a huge problem for him, however, because the sheet contained animals that were not considered clean (or kosher) according to Jewish dietary laws. At first, Peter refused to do as he was told. Then the voice told Peter, "What God has made clean, do not call common" (v. 15). The vision repeated twice more. Luke then tells us,

> While Peter was pondering the vision, the Spirit said to him, "Behold, three men are looking for you. Rise and go down and accompany them without hesitation, for I have sent them" (vv. 19–20).

The messengers came and stayed the night, and in the morning, Peter and some other believers went with them to Caesarea (v. 23).

In anticipation of Peter's arrival, Cornelius gathered a small group of people in his home. Peter arrived and told the group about the Good News of Jesus Christ. While the disciple was preaching, something incredible happened:

> The Holy Spirit fell on all who heard the word. And the believers from among the circumcised who had come with Peter were amazed, because the gift of the Holy Spirit was poured out even on the Gentiles. For they were hearing them speaking in tongues and extolling God (v. 44–46).

I like to call this "one-stop shopping," because the Gentiles gathered at Cornelius's house heard the message Peter presented, believed in Jesus, and received the baptism in the Holy Spirit.

Unlike the account of the Samaritans, who only received the Holy Spirit, Luke says, "the gift of the Holy Spirit was poured out" on the Roman Gentiles, *and* they received spiritual utterance. This new event completely changed the previous Jewish paradigm. For the Jewish believers, it would have been shocking, but they would also have remembered the prophetic words of Joel that promised the Spirit would be poured out on *all* flesh.

THE DISCIPLES AT EPHESUS

In Acts 19, the apostle Paul arrived at Ephesus. He located about 12 followers of Jesus there and asked them this question: "Did you receive the Holy Spirit when you believed?" They answered that they had not (Acts 19:2).

We can deductively reason that Paul would not have asked this question if it were a theological truth that the Holy Spirit automatically begins to dwell within people when they are born again and nothing more is necessary. He would have asked a different question, such as, "Do you believe in the Lord Jesus Christ?" Logically, if they had answered that they did, then that would be the end of the matter. However, Luke says these believers in Ephesus were "disciples," which means they were followers of Jesus. Therefore, Paul didn't need to ask them *if* they believed but instead used the clause "*when you believed.*"

Consider these believers' full answer to Paul's question: "No, we have not even heard that there is a Holy Spirit" (Acts 19:2). Wait a minute! Don't pass over their response too quickly.

They were disciples, but they had never heard there was the Holy Spirit? It's fairly astounding that they reached this point in their relationship with Jesus and had not heard of the Spirit. The Spirit of God was known in the Old Testament, and Jesus had promised the Spirit would come. How did they not know?

Paul then asked these disciples, "Into what then were you baptized?" (Acts 19:3). Why would he ask that question? Because water baptism was in the name of the Father, the Son, *and the Holy Spirit.* So if they were baptized, they would have probably heard that phrase, right? They replied, "Into John's baptism" (v. 3). Okay, now, we're getting the fuller picture.

Look at the rest of the story:

> Paul said, "John baptized with the baptism of repentance, telling people to believe in the one who was to come after him, that is, Jesus." On hearing this, they were baptized in the name of the Lord Jesus. And when Paul had laid his hands on them, the Holy Spirit came on them, and they began speaking in tongues and prophesying (Acts 19:4–6).

From this passage, we can see that these disciples were a little uninformed. They had been baptized in John's baptism, which was a baptism of repentance. They had come that far. They had believed Jesus was the Messiah. If I were guessing, then I would think they had originally heard John the Baptist preaching when they were in Jerusalem, celebrating one of the feasts. They may have even heard the gospel of Jesus shortly after the Resurrection and believed in it, meaning they believed the Messiah had come, and then they returned home. Enter the apostle Paul with the rest of the story.

When these men received the Holy Spirit, what was the result? They spoke in tongues, or they received a spiritual utterance. And they did something else—they prophesied. At this point, a pattern is emerging in the New Testament. Individuals received the baptism in the Holy Spirit after salvation. The baptism in the Holy Spirit does not replace salvation. It is something in addition to it. Furthermore, on at least two occasions, spiritual utterance was evident as the individuals received the Holy Spirit.

> *The baptism in the Holy Spirit does not replace salvation. It is something in addition to it.*

Typically, when people get saved, they are then baptized in water as followers of Jesus. Baptism doesn't save them; it is an act of obedience. Baptism in the Holy Spirit is also subsequent to salvation. Most of the time, people who receive it pursue it. The disciples waited in the upper room looking for the promise of the Father in obedience to Jesus' instruction. It was at least 50 days after they had received the indwelling Holy Spirit at salvation that they received the Spirit baptism that came upon them on the day of Pentecost. In the example of Cornelius and the people who were with him, they received the infilling of the Holy Spirit while Peter was preaching, and they began speaking in tongues and prophesying. And something supernatural occurred when Peter and John laid hands on the Samaritans. Simon the sorcerer's interest in buying the power from Peter and John indicates that something dynamic happened there as well.

THE APOSTLE PAUL

In Acts 9, the apostle Paul is converted, but we first meet him by the name Saul at the close of Acts 7. Saul is mentioned as the young man at whose feet the "witnesses laid down their garments" at the stoning of Stephen (Acts 7:58). Saul had approved of Stephen's execution (see Acts 8:1).

Saul was a young Jew of the Pharisee sect who saw the Church exploding in power. He began zealously persecuting the Church. Luke writes, "Saul was ravaging the church, and entering house after house, he dragged off men and women and committed them to prison" (Acts 8:3). "Still breathing threats and murder against the disciples of the Lord," Saul secured letters to deliver to the synagogues in Damascus that would permit him to continue his arrests (see Acts 9:1–2).

While Saul was traveling to Damascus, he met Jesus on the road. It was like the spotlight from a police helicopter chasing a robber at night, only many times brighter. This vivid light from heaven was so brilliant that it knocked Saul off his horse and blinded him.

> And falling to the ground, he heard a voice saying to him, "Saul, Saul, why are you persecuting me?" And he said, "Who are you, Lord?" And he said, "I am Jesus, whom you are persecuting. But rise and enter the city, and you will be told what you are to do" (Acts 9:4–6).

I'm sure that when Paul first heard this voice, his mind scanned through all the stories he had been taught from the Hebrew

Scriptures. He would have remembered Moses and the burning bush or recalled the angels who appeared to Joshua. Can you imagine his shock when he heard, "I am Jesus"?

From that moment, everything Saul had ever known changed. He obeyed the Lord's instructions to go into the city, but he needed the help of those traveling with him because he was temporarily blinded. Meanwhile, God spoke to a man named Ananias, a follower of Jesus in Damascus. He told Ananias to go to Saul, "for he is a chosen instrument of mine to carry my name" (Acts 9:15). Though he protested at first, Ananias went to the place where Saul was staying, laid his hands on him, and said,

> Brother Saul, the Lord Jesus who appeared to you on the road by which you came has sent me so that you may regain your sight and be filled with the Holy Spirit (Acts 9:17).

Immediately, Saul was healed, receiving back his sight.

So when was Saul saved? I believe the text is clear that it was on the road to Damascus, because he immediately began obeying Jesus. And according to the words of Ananias, he was to pray for Saul's sight to be restored and for Saul to be filled with the Holy Spirit. Luke does record that Saul received his sight again. The text does not tell us definitively how Paul received the Spirit, but I don't think it's too much of a reach to assume he was filled with the Spirit simultaneous to regaining his sight.

We also know that Saul, who was also called Paul by his Gentile audience, later asked the disciples at Ephesus whether they had received the Holy Spirit. He placed his hands upon them, and they were baptized in the Holy Spirit. To the believers in Corinth, Paul wrote, "I thank God that I speak in tongues more than all of you" (1 Corinthians 14:18). It's safe to conclude Paul had the experience of being filled with the Holy Spirit or baptized in the Holy Spirit. Even if it isn't explicit in the text, the pattern that emerges in Acts is one in which people are saved, then baptized in the Holy Spirit, and then given the ability to speak in tongues.

> *The pattern that emerges in Acts is one in which people are saved, then baptized in the Holy Spirit, and then given the ability to speak in tongues.*

THE CRITERIA AND THE PATTERN

Back on the day of Pentecost in Acts 2, 120 followers of Jesus received the baptism in the Holy Spirit, and they spoke in spiritual languages. Then, Peter stood and boldly proclaimed the Good News. When he finished his sermon, he and the apostles were asked, "Brothers, what shall we do?" (Acts 2:37).

And Peter said to them, "Repent and be baptized every one of you in the name of Jesus Christ for the forgiveness of your sins, and you will receive the gift of the Holy Spirit. For the promise is for you and for your children and for all who are far off, everyone whom the Lord our God calls to himself" (Acts 2:38–39).

Peter gave the criteria, which I'll put in my own words: "Here is what you need to do. First, you need to repent and be saved. Next, you need to be baptized in the name of Jesus. And then you will receive the gift of the Holy Spirit." Lastly, Peter told them for whom the gift was made available. In essence, he said the gift or the promise of the Father was for "you and for your children and for all who are far off, everyone whom the Lord our God will call to himself."

For whom did Peter say the promise of the Spirit was given? *Everyone.* God did not limit it to a certain group, location, or generation. It is for *you.* Why is that point important? Because there are a lot of people who say, "Oh no, no. That was a unique thing God did one time and in one place." They will say, "He only did that for the apostles and the first generation of believers," or "He did that until there was the closing of the canon when the Scripture was completed, and now He doesn't do that anymore because everything the Holy Spirit has to say is in the Bible."

As we have just seen, the Bible doesn't confirm any of those statements. The book of Acts shows us a pattern. You may be wondering, *If that pattern is clearly evident, then why are so many Christians not teaching it, talking about it, or believing in it?* Well, in case you didn't know, it's a *red-hot* topic for sure. When we talk about the *outflow of the overflow* that comes as a result of the infilling of the Holy Spirit, we mean the supernatural gifts of the Holy Spirit being manifested in our present day. However, there seems to be one gift in particular that offends the human sensibilities more than any other. And it is the gift of spiritual utterance—*speaking in tongues.*

THE OUTFLOW OF THE OVERFLOW

That pattern we have witnessed in the Acts is this: when people were baptized in the Holy Spirit, there was a corresponding outflow of the overflow, which means spiritual gifts followed the infilling. I want to return to the discussion of the Greek word *baptizo* to further our understanding. As I said before, *baptizo* means to submerge, to overwhelm, to saturate, and to take something under the water. That overflow can't happen to us without something coming up inside of us that needs to be released. This experience explains why so often people who are being water baptized come up praising God or sometimes even speaking in tongues. This kind of response follows the Acts pattern. The outpouring on the day of Pentecost definitively demonstrated that when the Holy Spirit comes upon someone, the overflow of that has an expression. God gave those early disciples the gift of spiritual utterance, which then flowed out in praise toward Him in tongues.

I am often asked why God chose to give the gift of speaking in tongues. I typically answer in this way: "I believe God picked speaking in tongues because if He can open your mind and spirit, then it is like priming the pump for all the other gifts to flow." I admit that too few of us who are pastors, including those of us in Spirit-empowered churches, teach about the beauty of spiritual utterance; instead, we get distracted by the controversy surrounding it. I don't believe any other gift of the Holy Spirit has as much controversy surrounding it in the body of Christ than the gift of tongues or spiritual utterance. For some, it is the proof of the infilling of the Holy Spirit. For others, it may have happened in the first century but is now an extinct manifestation that God only did for a limited time before the canon of Scripture was complete. This theological position is called *cessationism*, meaning that the gifts of the Holy Spirit *ceased* at some point not long after the early apostles died.

We need to begin to see tongues or spiritual utterance as not simply proof of the infilling of the Holy Spirit but as a privilege and promise to every believer. In every case of the infilling of the Holy Spirit in the book of Acts, speaking in tongues was explicitly mentioned or, at the very least, implied. Jesus told His disciples not to leave Jerusalem until they had received the promise of the Father. Why, then, would any believer think we can live dynamic, powerful, Spirit-empowered lives and be effective witnesses for Jesus in our generation without the Holy Spirit? Why would we think we can do something Jesus clearly said the disciples couldn't do?

I am convinced that rather than focusing on the controversy or tripping over the embarrassment people believe they may feel if they receive and use the gift of tongues, we need to see, teach, and preach about the beauty, power, and blessing of this gift. As I mentioned at the beginning of this chapter, I don't know for certain what happened when that Orthodox Jewish man heard me praying in tongues for his nation and people, but I fully believe something transpired. I think Jesus would say the following to every believer today: I love you. You're saved and on your way to heaven, but I have this wonderful gift, this empowerment, that I want to give you. I want to clothe you with power from on high. I have this gift of the Holy Spirit. He's the One who dwells within you today, and He has dynamic gifts He wants to unload supernaturally through your life. These gifts will help you in your prayer life with Me, and they're going to take your relationship with the Father to a whole new level. And then you're going to be fully empowered to be My witnesses.

One of the devil's most sinister tactics is to use the subject of tongues to create controversy in the body of Christ. The enemy knows that if he can keep the Church weak and powerless, then we will not fulfill the Great Commission in our present day.

I want everything God has for me. I also want you to desire everything God has for you. We need the power of the Holy Spirit. The promise of the Father is a gift for everyone—and everyone means *you*.

The promise of the Father is a gift for everyone—and everyone means you.

Father, we don't necessarily understand all that we read in the book of Acts. But something about those events and the outpouring of Your Spirit stirs us. It creates a hunger and a thirst for everything You have for us. We want to impact our generation with the gospel. We want to see Your Kingdom on earth just as it is in heaven. Lord, we confess any doubt in us regarding the work of Your Holy Spirit. Please help our unbelief and increase our faith. In Jesus' name, Amen.

CHAPTER 7

STUDY GUIDE

THE BOOK OF Acts reveals a clear pattern in the experiences of believers in the early church. Disciples with different backgrounds had different experiences, but in all cases, there was a corresponding outflow of spiritual gifts following the infilling. In every instance of the infilling of the Holy Spirit, speaking in tongues was either explicitly mentioned or at least implied. The promise of the Father is a gift for everyone.

REVIEW

1. Why did Simon the sorcerer desire the gifts he saw the Samaritans receive when they were baptized in the Holy Spirit?
2. What was wrong with the baptism the followers of Jesus at Ephesus had received? How did Paul correct them? What does this clearly teach about the relationship between salvation and the timing of the baptism in the Holy Spirit?
3. For whom is the promise of the Holy Spirit given?

REFLECTION

1. What were you taught about the timing of salvation and the baptism in the Holy Spirit?

2. Have you been baptized in the Holy Spirit? Have you received any spiritual gifts? If so, which ones?
3. Why do you think the devil uses the issue of miraculous spiritual gifts, especially the gift of tongues, to create controversy in the Church?

CHAPTER 8

FOR YOU

And when they had prayed, the place in which they were gathered together was shaken, and they were all filled with the Holy Spirit and continued to speak the word of God with boldness.

—Acts 4:31

I SUPPOSE I SHOULD HAVE GOTTEN a clue when I first went to my Bible college's bookstore and picked up one of the textbooks for my theology class. The title on the cover screamed at me. It directly stated that the Bible college's founder thought he knew where speaking in tongues originated, and it wasn't in heaven! Maybe it was my youthful naiveté, my inexperienced smugness, or my innocent ignorance, but all I can remember was thinking, *Hmm, this is probably going to be challenging.*

Remember when I told you earlier that I was kicked out of Bible college? Well, this was that college. Even so, my experience was not a complete loss. I met some students and teachers who were godly people. I could tell they loved the Bible. I could see they loved Jesus. Sadly, I also discovered that the subject of speaking in tongues was a lightning rod, and it really seemed to upset them.

At first, it was great to be in a Christian environment with people who didn't see everything exactly the same way I did. I engaged in several debates with them about a number of issues.

For the first year and a half, the school helped me to deconstruct many of my own beliefs. It was as if I were an old truck that had its motor torn out and rebuilt again. I was also able to explore and reevaluate my beliefs regarding the Holy Spirit, including many of the issues I've already covered in this book. As a whole, I came out of the experience stronger in my faith regarding the miraculous work of the Holy Spirit.

The college's leadership soon heard about my thoughts on the Holy Spirit and His supernatural work in believers. They developed a plan to help me "see the light" and put me in the same dorm room as the son of a prominent leader in the college. That may have been a big mistake—on their part. Soon, my new roommate grew intrigued with my prayer life and church experience. One week, he asked if he could attend church with me, so I took him the following Sunday. It was a small Pentecostal church, and from the very beginning of the service, I could see my roommate was fascinated. This was his first experience with a Pentecostal worship service, and he was waiting for all the crazy things he had been told would happen during the service. Later, I learned that he fully expected to see people swing from the chandeliers, froth at the mouth, and go slithering across the floor like snakes. But none of that happened.

Much to his own surprise, my roommate was deeply moved during the service. And that initial experience began a meaningful and progressive conversation between the two of us. In fact, we increased in our knowledge and respect for each other to the point where he eventually felt comfortable enough to ask me,

"Do you speak in tongues?"

"Yes, every day," I answered.

"Really? Can I hear?"

He put me on the spot, yet I felt he was sincere, so I replied,

"I'm going to be praying in a little while. You're welcome
to read your Bible and pray along. You might catch me
praying stuff in the Spirit."

After a little while, we sat together on our dorm room floor. I
began to read my Bible with intermittent prayer. At one point,
I began to pray in tongues, and he heard me. He looked up at
me with a flushed face and asked,

"Is that it?"

"Yeah, that's it."

He didn't say anything else to me that day, but a few days
later, he approached the subject again.

"It's not as weird as I thought."

"What did you expect?" I asked.

"I don't know. Maybe I was expecting you to roll around on
the floor or something."

My roommate's hunger for the things of the Spirit grew after
that. In fact, he asked me if he could pray in the Spirit like I had
done. I replied that this gift was available for all who believed.
That day, I prayed with him. I laid my hands on him, and he
was filled with the Holy Spirit and began speaking in tongues.
That was the beginning of the end for me at that Bible college.

Soon after, my roommate told his father what happened. When
the time came for me to register for classes the following
semester, I was told to go see his father first. As I sat in the

office of the Dean of students, he said to me, "You know, Lee, I think you're not going to change us, and we're not going to change you. I think it's better if you just go to a different institution." And that was that.

I recognize there are many God-fearing, Jesus-loving brothers and sisters in the body of Christ who do not believe in the gifts or the ministry of the Holy Spirit. From the beginning of this study, I have acknowledged this fact. From my perspective, speaking in tongues should be an open-handed issue, which means I don't believe it necessitates we part fellowship over it. I endeavor to remain in fellowship with all who believe in Jesus. However, I would also say that it shouldn't be an issue we won't or can't talk about. The apostle Paul asked the Ephesian disciples: "Did you receive the Holy Spirit when you believed?" (Acts 19:2). And Jesus told His disciples not to leave the city of Jerusalem without the promise of the Father.

I encourage you to be faithful to you in this moment wherever you are on this issue. I promise not to embarrass or harass you. I simply want to ask you this question: did you receive the Holy Spirit when you believed? If not, then I implore you to wait for Him. Don't leave without Him, because His beneficial promise is for you.

BENEFITS OF SPEAKING IN TONGUES

Speaking in tongues is the ability to pray in a spiritual language that has not been learned or is not known by the person praying. When the New Testament uses the phrase "praying in the Spirit," it typically refers to speaking in tongues. Jude encourages believers to build themselves up "in your most holy faith and praying in the Holy Spirit" (Jude 20). The apostle Paul wrote to the Ephesians,

> In all circumstances take up the shield of faith, with which you can extinguish all the flaming darts of the evil one; and take the helmet of salvation, and the sword of the Spirit, which is the word of God, **praying at all times in the Spirit, with all prayer and supplication**. To that end, keep alert with all perseverance, making supplication for all the saints (Ephesians 6:16–18, emphasis added).

In these New Testament passages, we see two of the benefits of speaking in tongues: *private edification* and *spiritual preparedness*. Through Spirit-empowered and Spirit-directed prayer, we are able to encourage ourselves in faith, and we prepare ourselves for spiritual battle. We are spiritually armed as we pray in the Spirit.

I admit that I don't know a lot about cars, but I do know a car requires energy to make the motor run. That energy is produced by the alternator, which creates electricity that flows through the car. However, before the alternator can generate energy, a battery has to jump it. When I turn the key, the battery gives a little *hummm*, the car starts—*vroom*—and then the generator takes it from there.

If the generator (the alternator) is bad, then it will fry the battery. If the battery doesn't work, then the car will not start. (I think I got that right, but I'll pause to apologize right now to any mechanics reading this book.) This picture of an alternator that is spinning and creating energy for the car to run is what

I think it means to build yourself up in your most holy faith. Praying in tongues generates energy and power.

> *Praying in tongues generates energy and power.*

When you pray in the Spirit, you build yourself up spiritually. You edify and prepare yourself spiritually. "Praying at all times in the Spirit" is part of putting on "the whole armor of God" (Ephesians 6:11). You're strengthening yourself. It's as if you are pumping iron in the Spirit so that you will become stronger. The apostle Paul wrote, "The one who speaks in a tongue builds up himself" (1 Corinthians 14:4).

A third benefit of praying in tongues is *the generation of certain dynamics that release other spiritual gifts.* It helps us open up to the further flow of the Spirit's activity in our lives. It's like sowing to the Spirit (see Galatians 6:8).

The apostle Paul instructs believers to "pursue love, and earnestly desire the spiritual gifts" (1 Corinthians 14:1). Praying in the Spirit activates certain dynamics in our pursuit. And if God designed the gifts of the Spirit, including the gift of tongues, and wants us to pursue them, then we should take a closer look, open our hearts, and be receptive to those gifts that will strengthen our relationship with Him and help us fulfill the Great Commission.

PRAYING IN TONGUES

There are some additional things you should understand about praying in tongues.

DIRECTED TOWARD GOD

First, when we pray in tongues, our prayer is directed toward God, which means we're praying to God. The apostle Paul wrote to the Corinthians, "For one who speaks in a tongue speaks not to men but to God; for no one understands him, but he utters mysteries in the Spirit" (1 Corinthians 14:2). When you pray in tongues, you're praying directly to God, but you may not know the content of the prayer because the Holy Spirit is praying through you to the Father. When I was praying in tongues next to the Orthodox Jewish man at the Wailing Wall, my heart was reaching out to the Father and interceding for the salvation of the nation of Israel, but I didn't know what I was saying in tongues.

Maybe you're hesitant to accept what I am saying. You might be thinking, *What I don't like about this whole tongues thing is I will feel out of control.* I would respond that what you are thinking is exactly true. We do have control issues. You may also be thinking, *Well, what good does it do me if I can't understand what I'm saying?* I would respond again that you may not know what you're praying, but the Spirit does. And He prays to the Father on your behalf.

I believe one of the reasons why God gave this gift to us as believers was so He could bypass our natural minds. Paul notes that our minds are set on the flesh and are hostile to God (see Romans 8:7). We are unable to receive the things of the Spirit with our natural thinking. Paul writes, "For if I pray in a tongue, my spirit prays but my mind is unfruitful" (1 Corinthians 14:14). This verse does not mean we should stop praying with our intellect or our own languages, because in the next verse Paul says, "I will pray with the spirit, and I will also pray with the understanding" (1 Corinthians 14:15 NKJV). When I pray with understanding, I pray out of my emotions and thoughts. I pour out everything I can before the Lord based on my knowledge, intellect, and perspective. It is good and necessary for me to pray this way.

On the other hand, when I pray in the Spirit, the Holy Spirit prays on my behalf. He knows things past, present, and future. In fact, the Holy Spirit knows everything. He is aware of what makes me tick, and He can track what is going on in my life as well as in the world around me. The Holy Spirit knows every cell in my body, the way I process life, and what the will of the Father is for me. He also knows what is happening in the spiritual realm. The Holy Spirit is our constant bridge, bypassing the natural barriers of our minds where doubt and unbelief get in the way. He is the conduit that enables us to pray straight to the Father from our spirits.

PRAYING MYSTERIES

Second, praying in tongues is praying mysteries. That is the other thing Paul reveals in 1 Corinthians 14:2. We don't know what lies ahead in God's agenda, but the Holy Spirit does. Often, we don't even know exactly how to direct our prayers. Paul wrote,

> Likewise the Spirit helps us in our weakness. For we do not know what to pray for as we ought, but the Spirit himself intercedes for us with groanings too deep for words (Romans 8:26).

Sometimes we may feel a weightiness or burden about something or someone in our lives, but we aren't certain of the best way to pray in response. So what do we do? In those times, we pray in tongues and let the Spirit pray through us. In our weakness or inability, the Holy Spirit helps us to pray through those things that are mysteries to us but not to Him.

Have you ever prayed and felt as if there were something down deep inside that needed to be expressed? The best word I can think of to describe that is a *groan*. Sometimes we simply have no words to describe what is going on inside us or around us. As we begin to pray in tongues in moments such as these, the Holy Spirit begins to release those groans from the deepest parts of us. In those times, we can be confident that the Holy Spirit is speaking to the Father on our behalf, even though we are unable to form words for what is in our minds and hearts.

THE ONE WHO INTERCEDES

Third, when we pray in tongues, the Holy Spirit intercedes for us based on God's will. The apostle Paul confirms this truth when he writes, "The Spirit intercedes for the saints according to the will of God" (Romans 8:27). God the Father and God the Holy Spirit have an agreement with God the Son. Jesus paid for your sins on the cross as a means to accomplish God's purpose for your life, and the Holy Spirit has been sent to lead and guide you in every step so that you will fulfill it. Every time you pray in the Spirit, there is a conversation among the Persons of the

Trinity. Think of it as a divine conference or board meeting as God considers you and your destiny.

Every time you pray in the Spirit, there is a conversation among the Persons of the Trinity.

PERSONAL PRAYER LANGUAGE

Fourth, Paul encouraged every believer to pursue a personal prayer language. Earlier in this chapter, I discussed the benefits of speaking in tongues and showed the way Paul admonished believers to pursue the gifts. Furthermore, he said,

> Now I want you all to speak in tongues, but even more to prophesy. The one who prophesies is greater than the one who speaks in tongues, unless someone interprets, so that the church may be built up (1 Corinthians 14:5).

You see, Paul wanted everyone to speak in tongues, and it is a gift available to everyone. He also wanted all to prophesy, because prophecy builds up the Church. Generally, tongues benefits the individual believer, whereas prophecy helps the Church as a whole. Both gifts build up, encourage, and strengthen.

Finally, Jesus said speaking in tongues would be a sign that would accompany believers:

> And he said to them, "Go into all the world and proclaim the gospel to the whole creation. Whoever believes and is

baptized will be saved, but whoever does not believe will be condemned. And these signs will accompany those who believe: in my name they will cast out demons; they will speak in new tongues; they will pick up serpents with their hands; and if they drink any deadly poison, it will not hurt them; they will lay their hands on the sick, and they will recover" (Mark 16:15–18).

Jesus was saying, "Do you want to know who believes in Me? These are the things they will do." If we say we are believers, then these are the things God will miraculously enable us to do, and tucked away in His words is this important phrase: "they will speak in new tongues."

OBSTACLES TO RECEIVING THE GIFT OF TONGUES

Several things can keep us from receiving spiritual utterance or the gift of tongues.

IGNORANCE

The first obstacle is ignorance. We cannot receive something if we don't know it has been provided for us. The prophet Hosea said God's people "are destroyed for lack of knowledge" (Hosea 4:6). What we don't know *can* hurt us, and it can limit our ability to walk in all that God has for us. It's important for you to know what God has made available to you through the Holy Spirit, and He has made speaking in tongues available to you.

RELIGIOUS TRADITION

A second obstacle is religious tradition. The story I told about my Bible college experience at the opening of this chapter illustrates this truth. I believe religious tradition is often one of the most stubborn impediments to someone receiving the gift of tongues. A person won't pursue something they don't believe is right.

Early in Radiant Church's journey, we met in a school and needed to baptize several people who had been saved. At the time, it was winter, and we didn't have our own baptistry. I decided I would contact some of the other local churches and request to use their baptism facilities. One such church was in Kalamazoo. I reached someone who was in charge of the church's facilities and asked if we could use their baptistry. Of course, as part of that conversation, I told him I was pastoring a fairly new church plant. His immediate response shocked me.

> He said, "I'm sorry. We only let Christian churches use our facilities."
> "Excuse me, what do you mean by that?" I was immediately taken aback and actually felt a little lost. I was puzzled and wondering what I might have said to make him think we weren't Christians.
> "Well, you believe in speaking in tongues, don't you?"
> "That's right." I understood the issue then and decided not to let it go, "And so did Paul," I retorted.
> "We believe that tongues is actually demonic." It was the last thing he said to me.

I quickly responded, "Well, thank you very much. I would
rather baptize people in a kiddie pool out in the backyard
in the middle of November then."

What was his problem? (And I don't mean that as a flippant
question.) His problem actually came down to his religious
tradition. Jesus told the Pharisees that they made "the word
of God of no effect through [their] tradition which [they had]
handed down" (Mark 7:13 NKJV). Jesus was saying their traditions actually canceled out the power of Scripture in their
lives. I really want you to understand the importance of what
Jesus said: Anything in our lives that is influenced by religious
tradition as opposed to Scripture becomes an obstacle to the
will of God being accomplished in our lives. Religious tradition
becomes a millstone that weighs us down and keeps us down. It
can diminish the potency of God's promises for us.

> *Anything in our lives that is influenced*
> *by religious tradition as opposed*
> *to Scripture becomes an obstacle*
> *to the will of God being*
> *accomplished in our lives.*

HARDENED HEARTS

The third obstacle to receiving the gift of tongues is a hardened
heart. You cannot receive something if you are offended by it
or resistant to it. Have you ever been offended by the issue of
speaking in tongues? Let me ask it another way: has someone

who spoke in tongues offended you? Perhaps you've had a negative experience with someone, and it was somehow related to speaking in tongues or the baptism in the Holy Spirit. Or you may simply be put off by speaking in tongues in general, because it seems strange or weird to you. Could it be that you have made a vow such as, "God, You can have all of me. I'll do what You want me to do, but I don't want to do *that*"? "That" could represent anything from speaking in tongues to missionary service or becoming a pastor. These types of vows, however, create a layer of callousness over your soul that separates you from God's plans for you. The Holy Spirit will prompt you, lead you, and invite you to receive, but you can also create a barrier or limitation to what God wants for you when you harden your heart both to the gift and its Giver.

DOUBT AND UNBELIEF

The fourth obstacle is doubt and unbelief. You will not be able to receive by faith what you doubt to be true. The writer of Hebrews says, "Without faith *it is* impossible to please *Him*, for he who comes to God must believe that He is, and *that* He is a rewarder of those who diligently seek Him" (Hebrews 11:6 NKJV). So you have to believe God is and that He will give you what He has promised to give you. You must believe in order to receive. If you want to overcome this obstacle, then you must read the Word, hear the Word, and pray in faith. Paul writes, "Faith comes from hearing, and hearing through the word of Christ" (Romans 10:17).

FEAR

Finally, fear is a formidable obstacle. Fear is a robber, and it will try to steal from you. It will speak lies to you and will tell you that if you really open up, then you won't get what you asked for—that you may even receive something bad instead. Sometimes we have more faith in the devil to do bad supernatural things in our lives than we have for our heavenly Father to do good supernatural things in our lives. But Jesus said,

> What father among you, if his son asks for a fish, will instead of a fish give him a serpent; or if he asks for an egg, will give him a scorpion? If you then, who are evil, know how to give good gifts to your children, how much more will your heavenly Father give the Holy Spirit to those who ask him! (Luke 11:11–13).

You can trust God and His promises. He is a good Father. This promise of the Father is available to you if you have the courage to receive it. You will need the childlike mentality that says, "If my Dad has given me a promise, then He's going to come through. And my Dad gives good gifts!" And when it comes to the gift of the Holy Spirit—His baptism and speaking in tongues—we should be like little children waking up on Christmas morning,. knowing there are presents to be had. We should run to the gift and its Giver.

RECEIVING THE BAPTISM
IN THE HOLY SPIRIT
AND YOUR PRAYER LANGUAGE

If you want to experience this Spirit-driven life and follow the pattern of Jesus and the apostles, then you will need the infilling of the Holy Spirit. You need the baptism. Here are some of the things I have found helpful in receiving the baptism in the Holy Spirit with the gift of tongues.

- *Be convinced.* Allow the strong, biblical case for the baptism in the Holy Spirit to convince your heart that it's the will of God for you. It is the promise of the Father—for you.
- *Prepare your heart.* Focus on the Father's promise to you. Open your heart to receive it.
- *Ask the Father.* Believe He will baptize you with the Holy Spirit. When you believe, you receive. Remember that it's a gift, and it's from Him to you.
- *Create an environment of worship.* Oftentimes, your heart will be awakened to the glory and goodness of God during worship. It is the place where you will be most sensitive and receptive to the moving of the Spirit in your life. As you worship, you will be creating a spiritual environment for the Lord to come, to be enthroned, to speak, and to empower you. So worship God. One tool to help you is to play worship music.
- *Ask someone who has received the Holy Spirit to lay their hands on you and pray with you.* Remember the pattern in the book of Acts? The laying on of hands is one of the fundamental, foundational doctrines of the Church. Impartation happens when believers lay hands on one another in prayer.

They impart a spiritual blessing, or they may even transmit authority from one person to another for service or leadership.

- *Ask the Holy Spirit to show you a picture of what it would look or sound like for you to be filled with the Holy Spirit and speak in tongues.* I believe this is a key. Your imagination, your mind's eye, is a gift from God. Most of the time, if you are not engaging your mind in this process, then it's as if your mind is like a blank screen, which can provide the perfect setup for the enemy to put something else on that screen to prevent you from receiving what the Father has promised you. To keep that from happening, ask the Holy Spirit, "Please show me a vision of what being baptized and speaking in tongues will look like for me. I want to be able to see it." The Lord will show you, and you will suddenly see yourself receiving and speaking.
- *Release it verbally.* Speaking is required, so open your mouth and speak. You have to release what has risen up in you because you are being saturated or baptized in the Holy Spirit.
- *Thank God for giving you a prayer language.* Stay in the moment and praise God. Thank Him for giving you His promise.
- *Steward well what He has given you.* Use your gift. Remember Paul told us in Ephesians 6:18 to pray at all times in the Spirit.
- *Pray for more.* Ask the Holy Spirit for more of Him—to continue to fill you to overflowing.

God, we're hungry for more of You. We want everything You have for us. Jesus, baptize and fill us with the Holy Spirit. Give us power and release a prayer language in us. We want to be witnesses, and we want to encounter You. Thank You, Lord, for this baptism. In Jesus' name, Amen.

CHAPTER 8

STUDY GUIDE

THE GIFT OF TONGUES is defined as the ability to pray in a spiritual language that has not been learned or is not known by the person praying. It is a controversial topic and was the cause for me getting kicked out of Bible college. There are numerous benefits to praying in tongues and having your own prayer language. It is a powerful tool of the Spirit that also encounters many obstacles to its acceptance. However, if you receive the baptism and infilling of the Holy Spirit, you can receive this gift.

REVIEW

1. What are three benefits of speaking in tongues?
2. To whom is speaking in tongues directed? What are we praying when speaking in tongues? Who intercedes in those prayers and on what basis?
3. What are some of the obstacles to receiving the gift of tongues?

REFLECTION

1. What was your first reaction to the idea of speaking in tongues? Why do you think you felt that way?
2. If you have been baptized in the Holy Spirit, have you received the gift of tongues? If not, why not?

3. If you have not been baptized in the Holy Spirit, how does the idea of the gift of speaking in tongues affect your decision?

WALKING IN THE POWER
OF THE HOLY SPIRIT

WALKING IN THE POWER OF THE HOLY SPIRIT

For this reason I bow my knees before the Father, from whom every family in heaven and on earth is named, that according to the riches of his glory he may grant you to be strengthened with power through his Spirit in your inner being.

—The apostle Paul in Ephesians 3:14–16

SEVERAL YEARS AGO, my wife, Jane, and I sat in our living room and talked about a young couple who were doing what most young couples do: struggling. This couple had started having children, and life was pressing down hard on them. There were more mouths to feed, more responsibilities to share, and more bills than ever before!

> I said, "Remember what it was like when we were young and had babies to feed and take care of? It was hard, Jane, remember?"
>
> Jane looked at me and said, "I think we're supposed to give our car away."
>
> "What? What in the world are you talking about?" I asked, not immediately connecting what she was saying to what we had been talking about.
>
> "I'm not sure. I just feel like the Lord wants us to give our car away."

Pausing for a moment, working through some of my resistance to what she had just said, I suddenly found myself responding, "You know what? I think you're right!" It had to have been God for me to get there so quickly.

The next thing we knew, both of us were bustling around to get our car ready so we could gift it to this young couple. Thankfully, we had already finished paying for it, so we didn't have a delay in giving it to them as a gift. We washed it, cleaned it inside and out, and had it ready in the driveway, waiting for its new owners.

I can't tell you just how much fun we had getting everything ready for the moment we would give this car to the couple. We called them and asked, "Hey, can you guys stop by for a minute?" We didn't tell them why, but they agreed to come, completely unaware of what awaited them.

Once we had them in the house, I found a way to get the husband to go outside with me, and then I invited him to take a ride with me in the car. I could see he was slightly confused, but he was gracious enough to play along. "Jump in the car. Let's go for a ride," I said. Then when I saw him move toward the passenger side of the car, I stopped him and said, "No, I mean you jump in the driver's seat!"

He looked at me like he didn't understand what I was telling him I wanted him to do or why I was asking him to drive.

"Can you drive it around the block?" I asked, giving him the key, all the while trying to contain my excitement.

He slid into the driver's seat, and I plopped down into the
front passenger's side. He started the car, and away we
went. From time to time, I would ask questions, such as,
"Does the car drive well? Does it handle well?"

"Oh, yeah. It drives really nice," he would respond matter-of-
factly.

After a short drive, we rounded my block and pulled back into
the driveway. As we got out of the car, I blurted out, "All
right, enjoy it."

"What? What do you mean?" he asked.

"It's yours. The car is yours."

He was both shocked and surprised. He exited the car and
followed me into the house. Then he told his wife that I had
just given them the car. She couldn't believe it either. Jane and
I went on to explain to them that this was a present from God,
because He was the One who asked us to give it to them. They
thanked us over and over again.

Finally, when they pulled out of our driveway, Jane and I were
beaming. This experience was one of the greatest joys we have
ever had of being led together by the Holy Spirit, of partnering
with Him. He allowed us to bless the lives of two of His kids.
Jane and I still get a kick out of it to this day!

You know, when we think about the gifts of the Holy Spirit, we
tend to think of all these supernaturally powerful experiences.
However, walking in the power of the Holy Spirit is simply
walking in step with Him. When He says, "I want you to do
this. I want you to do that," then we respond in obedience. I
encourage you to do what He says. You will find a joyful reward
in obeying His voice.

Walking in the power of the Holy Spirit
is simply walking in step with Him.

WALKING IN STEP
WITH THE HOLY SPIRIT

What does it look like to walk daily in the power of the Holy Spirit? Jesus and the apostles are our examples or patterns for living supernaturally natural lives. Most of the powerful encounters we discussed in the previous chapter, as well as the many others that are recorded in the book of Acts, happened in the marketplace, in homes, on the street, or somewhere outside the church walls. Supernatural, powerful things happened as Jesus and the apostles went about their everyday lives, walking with everyday people in everyday situations. The only difference that made them extraordinary is that they had the power of the Holy Spirit in them and upon them, and they were led by Him.

The apostle Paul wrote specifically about walking in the Spirit, and he made the point that this walk would keep us from living a life motivated by our flesh. He said,

> But I say, walk by the Spirit, and you will not gratify the desires of the flesh. For the desires of the flesh are against the Spirit, and the desires of the Spirit are against the flesh, for these are opposed to each other, to keep you from doing the things you want to do. But if you are led by the Spirit, you are not under the law.... If we live by the Spirit, let us also keep in step with the Spirit (Galatians 5:16–18, 25).

Walking in the Spirit is a supernatural way of living, driven by the desires, abilities, and purposes of God. Paul recognized the internal battle that takes place in all of us. As long as we live in our bodies, we will have ongoing struggles and battles with the residue of our old, sinful natures. Our old natures try to pull us back into our ungodly patterns of thinking, ungodly attitudes, and ungodly appetites, all in this ungodly world.

> *Walking in the Spirit is a supernatural way of living, driven by the desires, abilities, and purposes of God.*

When you were born again, you received the indwelling of the Holy Spirit. I discussed earlier how the Holy Spirit works in your life to regenerate you, seal you, and free you. So the Spirit does all these things and gives you a new, divine nature. As the apostle Peter wrote,

> He has granted to us his precious and very great promises, so that through them you may become partakers of the divine nature, having escaped from the corruption that is in the world because of sinful desire (2 Peter 1:4).

You have received this new nature, yet the old, sinful nature still wants to act like it's alive. And you must battle against it with the power and strength of the Holy Spirit.

Looking back at what Paul said, he told us that the "desires of the Spirit are against the flesh." Did you realize the Holy

Spirit has desires for you? He has dreams and aspirations for you according to the will of the Father. The Holy Spirit continually intercedes on your behalf. He doesn't want your fleshly desires and cravings to pull you in all directions. The Holy Spirit is jealous for you. He desires for you to have a great adventure, which I've been referring to as the Spirit-empowered life. The Holy Spirit has things He wants you to do with Him, in Him, by Him, and through Him. He has desires that come expressly from the Father, and He wants to partner with you. And those desires are at enmity with the desires of your flesh.

So what can you do to get in step with the Holy Spirit? What do you need to do to make sure that old, sinful nature doesn't win any battles? The first thing to know is this: telling yourself over and over again that you're going to stop sinning won't work. Sin management is not a valid Christian discipline. Whenever you repeatedly tell yourself you're not going to do something, you're actually focusing on the thing you don't want to do. And the things you meditate on most are usually the things you will do the most.

In contrast, you need to strengthen your sensitivity to the Holy Spirit and obey Him so that the desires of your flesh will not be gratified. "Walk by the Spirit," Paul wrote, and "you will not gratify the desires of the flesh." You need to feed your spirit more than you feed your flesh, for whatever you feed the most becomes the strongest and most dominant. It follows the law of sowing and reaping. If you sow to your spirit things that are of the Holy Spirit, then you'll reap in your spirit those things of the Holy Spirit. Conversely, if you sow to your flesh things that are of the flesh, you'll reap in your flesh things that are of the flesh. Paul addressed this issue in Galatians 6.

Keeping in step with the Spirit will require you to become sensitive and led by "spiritual senses" rather than carnal triggers. All of us have things that can trigger us in carnal ways. For example, if someone pulls out in front of you while you're driving and makes you slam on your car's brakes, then it can carnally trigger you. Or your child might speak to you in a tone that can trigger you as well. Nevertheless, you don't want to be automatically set to trigger that way.

Instead, you want to develop your spiritual senses so they will respond to the Holy Spirit rather than your triggers. To do this, you will need to develop some good spiritual muscle memory. You recognize muscle memory when it comes to your flesh. As you work out a certain muscle group in your body, you begin to build muscle memory. As such, you hardly need to think about it. As you exercise those particular muscles, your muscles adapt to the resistance, and they become very skilled at whatever you're training them to do. In the same way, if you exercise praying in the Spirit, listening to the Spirit, and obeying what He tells you to do, then you will build spiritual muscle memory in those areas and will become skilled at those exercises. The writer of Hebrews says we can become "those who have their powers of discernment trained by constant practice to distinguish good from evil" (Hebrews 5:14). Spiritual practice is the way that we do it.

How can you know you're hearing the Holy Spirit? He does speak to us in a variety of ways. Sometimes we hear His voice in our minds. And what He tells us to do will never violate

His Word, His character, or His ways. He can reveal things in visions or dreams. Have you ever felt an internal nudge to go speak to or help someone? That is similar to what happened to Jane when she felt the Spirit tell her we needed to give our car to that young couple. She had an impression, and it changed our conversation. You may also have an idea or impression that will interrupt what you were doing or thinking. In Jane's case, she was carrying on a conversation with me when she spoke aloud the impression she was having. Trust me, we don't sit around thinking about how we can give away all our stuff. As she began to speak about her impression, I recognized in my spirit that I was okay with the idea of giving away our car. Any resistance I might typically have had just melted away. When we walk in the Spirit, we give God the opportunity to direct our steps, focus our eyes, and use us as vessels for His good pleasure.

> *When we walk in the Spirit, we give God the opportunity to direct our steps, focus our eyes, and use us as vessels for His good pleasure.*

Therefore, *walking in the Spirit* is a phrase we use to convey the idea of being tuned into His presence, His voice, and His promptings in our lives. We use our spiritual senses to listen to, see, and obey Him. All the while, we remain aware of His leadership in every moment of our lives. Walking in the Spirit is like anything else you might do; the more you practice it, the better you will become at doing it.

What walking in the Spirit looks like, then, is something super-naturally natural, meaning it happens in the normal course of our lives, but then something supernatural gets added to it. It's as normal as the apostle Peter walking down a city street, casually passing by people who are lying sick on mats. However, because he was walking in the Spirit, every time his shadow passed over them, they would be healed (see Acts 5:15–16). It looks as usual as Peter and John going to the Temple when a lame man begs them for money. But remember, they were walking in the Spirit. So Peter said, "Look at us.... I have no silver and gold, but what I do have I give to you. In the name of Jesus Christ of Nazareth, rise up and walk!" (Acts 3:4, 6). And immediately, the man got up and started walking and jumping. He was completely healed. Walking in the Spirit sometimes looks like plain walking, but then the Holy Spirit gets involved. He informs us and makes Himself available to work on our behalf and to empower us to minister to others.

NOT "ONE AND DONE"

"Jane, I think I'm having a heart attack. I've got to get off this plane!"

We had already boarded the airplane for departure from Australia. Suddenly, I suddenly felt completely trapped. The plane seemed to become more and more cramped by the second in my mind. I struggled to catch my breath.

"You can't get off this plane," she said, not yet comprehending my situation.

"I have to. I'm going to die! Something's wrong. I don't know what it is," I tried to relay what I was feeling without totally losing my composure.

We'd come to Australia for a time of ministry. I was already experiencing jetlag from our initial flight over and facing exhaustion. I admit I hadn't been taking care of myself like I should. It was 2006, and for several years I had avoiding taking a day off. Although I didn't realize it at the time, I was experiencing burnout and wrestling with depression.

As we sat on the plane at the departure gate, I struggled to keep it together. I closed my eyes and prayed, "God, You've got to save my life! You've got to do something."

Jane was sitting in the aisle seat, I was in the middle, and another man was by the window. I realized I was positioned in the worst possible seat possible for what I was experiencing. Jane was engrossed in a book by Francine Rivers titled *The Mark of the Lion*. All I could do was focus on my breathing while I fought to get through the feelings rushing through my mind and body. The plane seemed to be spinning, and the fuselage kept getting smaller and smaller. I felt more cramped and more helplessly trapped.

While I continued to pray, the man by the window looked over at Jane's book and said,

"Oh, you're reading Francine Rivers." I could tell by his speech he was an American.
"Oh, yeah. It's wonderful. It's a great book," Jane replied.
"Yeah. You must be a believer."

"Yeah, we both are,"
Jane said pointing to me and then back to herself. "We're
    both pastors."

As I observed their conversation, I came to a new realization:
*This man is a believer. I need to ask this man if he'll pray with us.
He just tipped us on to the fact that he's a believer.*

So immediately, I turned toward him with my request:

"Sir, I don't know what I'm experiencing, but I'm having—
    it feels like my chest is collapsing, and I'm scared. I'm
    nervous. I feel like I'm having a heart attack."
Looking at me, he gently responded, "Oh, no. You're having a
    panic attack."
"How do you know that?"
"I'm a psychiatrist. I'm from the University of Denver,
    and I've done my fellowship in depression and anxiety
    disorders. I've noticed your breathing. You're having an
    anxiety attack."

God knew. He was fully aware of what I would be experiencing,
and He ordered our steps and those of a Christian psychiatrist
from Colorado to meet on a plane in Australia. God even made
sure our seats would be next to each other. For the next two
hours, the psychiatrist gave me a free but incredibly valuable
counseling session, and he walked me through what I was
experiencing.

"When you get home," he told me, "here's what you need to
    do. You need to change your schedule. You need to follow
    up with a counselor."

This kind, godly man taught me some breathing exercises, and he and Jane prayed for me. Before long, I began to calm and breathe normally. In the middle of one of the most traumatic experience was one of the most intimate confirmations of the Lord's goodness to me that I have ever experienced. In one of my weakest moments, God let me know He was with me and He had ordered my steps. He not only sent one of His children but one who was a top expert.

You see, walking in the Spirit isn't about walking in triumph all the time. It is walking even in our human weakness. The Holy Spirit demonstrates His power by taking care of us. Even when our flesh reacts to our circumstances, God is working in us through His Holy Spirit.

I have now reached a very important point in our study. When you receive the baptism in the Holy Spirit and your prayer language, it's not as if you're "one and done." You can't say, "Okay, I've done that, and now I'll just move on." No, when you receive the baptism in the Holy Spirit, it is like a doorway you have stepped through, and on the other side is a new way of living. You are now living in a divine partnership with a living God. There is always more to come, and never "one and done."

Even more, the baptism in the Holy Spirit isn't a one-time event. God is calling you to be filled and refilled with the Holy Spirit every day of your life. This filling is what will give you the ability to walk continually in step and in the power of the Holy Spirit, exercising the gifts He wants to release in your life and using His power to share the fruit of the Spirit with others.

*God is calling you to be filled
and refilled with the Holy Spirit
every day of your life.*

Holy Spirit, create in us a greater awareness of Your presence. Strengthen our spiritual senses so we will recognize when You are speaking to and directing us. We want to walk in step with You. And we acknowledge that means we need to receive fresh baptisms and fillings, at different times in our lives. Fill us to overflowing again today, and may the overflow bless others for Your glory and honor. In Jesus' name, Amen.

STUDY GUIDE

WALKING IN THE SPIRIT is a supernatural way of living. It is not an easy thing to do, because as the apostle Paul noted in Galatians 5, our flesh and our spirit are constantly at war. "The desires of the Spirit are against the flesh." Even Paul, who was probably filled with the Spirit as much as anyone except Jesus, had to fight these temptations. Walking in the Spirit is a way to be tuned in to His presence, His voice, and His promptings in our lives. It is not about walking in triumph all the time. It is walking even in our human weakness.

REVIEW

1. Where do most of the "supernatural" encounters that demonstrate the power of the Holy Spirit in our lives occur? Why is this so?
2. What are the drivers of this supernatural way of living? How does that relate to the internal conflict of flesh and spirit?
3. How did my experience on the airplane in Australia demonstrate the leading of God and walking in the Spirit?

REFLECTION

1. What experiences have you had that reflected walking with God—either in yourself or others that you have observed? Explain.

2. Do you tend to focus on the things you shouldn't do and try to manage sin, or do you meditate on God's goodness and feed your spirit? If the former, how can you change that behavior?

3. What are some carnal triggers that can lead you away from walking in the Spirit? What weaknesses do you have that your flesh tends to react to?

USING YOUR SPIRITUAL GIFTS

So with yourselves, since you are eager for manifestations of the Spirit, strive to excel in building up the church.

—The apostle Paul in 1 Corinthians 14:12

SEVERAL YEARS AGO, I stood in the backyard of a home in Cuba that doubled as a house church. The husband and wife who co-pastored the church owned the property and the house where we were meeting. We had just finished a worship service when the wife, who was blind, approached me with an interpreter. Through her interpreter, she said, "I want you to pray for me for healing. I want God to heal my eyes. I want to be able to see the people I've pastored for the last 37 years." I then discovered she had lost her sight at a very young age.

I admit that I did not suddenly have a surge of faith, especially since I realized she had been blind for many years. I could see a white film covering her eyes. No, I had no great faith at the moment—but *she* had faith! So I proceeded to lay my hands on her and pray for her. I prayed each phrase slowly so the interpreter could repeat in Spanish what I was saying in English. I started, "Lord, would You just have mercy on this woman? Would You heal her eyes?"

Then I pulled my hands away, still clinging to the thread of faith I had for her healing. I did not expect to see what I saw.

At first, I had to blink again to check my own eyes. But there they were—brown eyes that were no longer clouded over! The wife began to exclaim excitedly in Spanish, "¡Puedo ver! ¡Puedo ver!" The translator kept repeating what she was saying into English: "I can see! I can see!"

Next, she turned away from me and began approaching different people in the crowd, commanding them, "¡Hable! "¡Hable!" At first, I didn't understand the significance of what she was saying. Then I realized she wanted different individuals to speak so she could match the voices she already recognized with the faces she had never before seen. Until that very moment, I had never really considered that she only knew the members of her church by the sounds of their voices.

That healing was one of the most profound miracles of my life. And here is the real truth: it had nothing to do with me. I was simply present and willing, and the Holy Spirit used me to pray for this woman. It was according to *her* faith that she received her sight!

SPIRITUAL GIFTS

The apostle Paul told the believers in Corinth that there was something very important he didn't want them to be ignorant about:

> Now concerning spiritual gifts, brothers, I do not want you to be uniformed. You know that when you were pagans you were led astray to mute idols, however you were led (1 Corinthians 12:1–2).

I find it amazing that teaching about spiritual gifts or manifestations of the Holy Spirit was very important to one of the founding fathers of the early church, yet so many denominations today don't believe those gifts are currently active or available for the Church. I'm with Paul, though, and this book is the School of the Spirit where we discuss such things.

Consider the Greek term that is translated *gifts*. It is the word *charisma(ta)*. It comes from the same root word that is translated *grace*. The word occurs 26 times in the New Testament. When we discuss "spiritual gifts," we're referring to supernatural manifestations of God's grace. I must point out that it's not earned—it's grace! Neither you nor I deserve it. There's no way we can buy it like Simon the sorcerer attempted to do. God deposits spiritual gifts in us by His grace and His grace alone.

When we discuss "spiritual gifts," we're referring to supernatural manifestations of God's grace.

Paul lists nine spiritual gifts in 1 Corinthians 12. Incidentally, there are also nine attributes of the fruit of the Spirit listed in Galatians 5:22–23. Nine is a number that represents grace. I will repeat that it is all of grace and all about grace. Here is the rest of what Paul had to say about these gifts:

> Therefore I want you to understand that no one speaking in the Spirit of God ever says "Jesus is accursed!" and no one can say "Jesus is Lord" except in the Holy Spirit.

Now there are varieties of gifts, but the same Spirit; and there are varieties of service, but the same Lord; and there are varieties of activities, but it is the same God who empowers them all in everyone. To each is given the manifestation of the Spirit for the common good. For to one is given through the Spirit the utterance of wisdom, and to another the utterance of knowledge according to the same Spirit, to another faith by the same Spirit, to another gifts of healing by the one Spirit, to another the working of miracles, to another prophecy, to another the ability to distinguish between spirits, to another various kinds of tongues, to another the interpretation of tongues. All of these are empowered by one and the same Spirit, who apportions to each one individually as he wills (1 Corinthians 12:3–11).

Notice that the last verse says, "All of these." Paul is saying that all the gifts he listed are for every one of us, subject to God's will and timing. A better translation would be "manifestations of the Spirit." But understand that all of these gifts are for every single believer.

If we think only certain people have certain gifts available to them, then we are mistaken. The truth is, you will operate with the Holy Spirit in a particular gift or couple of gifts at a time according to God's will for a particular situation; however, every gift is available to every believer all the time because the Holy Spirit is not distributing inanimate objects. In other words, these are not tools of the Spirit; they are actual manifestations of the Spirit. So you cannot have the Holy Spirit apart from all the manifestations of the Spirit being present, just as I could not have a conversation in person with you without you being present.

> *The gifts of the Spirit are not tools of the Spirit; they are actual manifestations of the Spirit.*

When we talk about walking in step with the Spirit, what we mean is that we are following very closely; we are hot on His heels. We want to be going wherever He is going. Remember, He is leading us. Understand that the Holy Spirit will never lead you away from ministry, serving others, your destiny, or your purpose. He's always leading you toward your purpose because He prays for you according to the will of the Father. The Holy Spirit will also equip you with every gift and empowerment you need at every stage and moment as you journey toward your purpose. You may not know exactly where you're going, but He will lead you where you need to go. The Holy Spirit will always take you in the right direction.

In general, I think most Americans focus on discovering their destinies. Instead of asking, "What is my destiny?" I believe we should ask, "What is my obedience?" If we simply live to be obedient to the Holy Spirit every day, then we'll be faithful and accepted. We will then fulfill our purpose. Although you may have some sense of your purpose or are aware of your calling, you still must obey the leadership of the Holy Spirit because you don't know the way there on your own.

Manifestations of the Holy Spirit open our senses to engage with the supernatural. When we are baptized in the Holy Spirit, we become open to the spiritual realm where God functions and operates. This spiritual realm is eternal, whereas the natural realm is temporal. Once we have stepped into the realm of the Spirit, which is governed by the dynamics of the Spirit, we will need to develop a whole new set of muscle reflexes. We will need to learn how to function within this realm because it is a whole new dynamic for us.

For the purposes of this study, I have grouped the spiritual gifts into three clusters. The first cluster includes the *revelatory gifts*, which are the word (or utterance) of wisdom, the word (or utterance) of knowledge, and discerning of spirits (or discernment). The second cluster is made up of the *power gifts,* such as faith, healing(s), and working of miracles. The third and final cluster consists of the *utterance or vocal gifts*, which are tongues, interpretation of tongues, and prophecy.

Before exploring each of these clusters of gifts, I first want to address our typical Western paradigm. In our culture, we typically want to outline everything or group things together as I just did. However, we need to realize that God doesn't operate that way. Remember, the Holy Spirit is like the wind. Our Western tendency is to compartmentalize these spiritual gifts or manifestations. We might say something like, "Okay, I'm operating right now in the gift of wisdom, and that's it." We are trained to expect straight lines and neat little boxes, but most of the time spiritual gifts work in conjunction with each other. Often, it's difficult for us to distinguish where one manifestation ends and the other begins. God works in a spectrum where colors bleed and blend into one another and are not easily defined, yet we still try to identify distinct colors, right? As I discuss the different clusters, try to see things outside of your Western paradigm and recognize that the gifts work in concert with each other.

REVELATORY GIFTS

We receive revelatory gifts as the Holy Spirit deposits information that we would not be able to obtain by way of human intellect or the human mind; rather, the information comes from the mind of Christ. Like all the other spiritual manifestations, these gifts are of supernatural origin. The Holy Spirit intends for us to communicate this information to someone on His behalf in order to strengthen or help that individual. Isaiah's prophecy regarding the Messiah highlights these gifts as manifestations of the Spirit:

> And the Spirit of the LORD shall rest upon him,
>> the Spirit of wisdom and understanding,
>> the Spirit of counsel and might,
>> the Spirit of knowledge and the fear of the LORD
> (Isaiah 11:2).

THE WORD OF WISDOM

The **word of wisdom** (or utterance of wisdom) is the ability to have insight into people and situations that is not obvious to a person using natural faculties, combined with an understanding of what to do and how to do it. For example, God can give you an infusion of wisdom directly from His heart. This ability is supernatural and enables someone to break through and change a situation, encourage the people involved, and bring about the will of God for them..

The word of wisdom includes not only the ability to see but also insight to apply the principles of God's Word to the practical matters of life. However, this ability comes through revelation and not by natural wisdom, understanding, or knowledge.

An example of the word of wisdom in the New Testament occurred at the Jerusalem council in Acts 15. According to this passage of Scripture, some men from Judea were telling new Gentile believers that they must adhere to Jewish customs in order to be a part of the Church. These men were known as Judaizers, specifically because they came from Judea. They told the male Gentile believers that they must be circumcised. The apostles and elders came together in a council in Jerusalem to weigh the matter. The apostle Peter stood up in the meeting and said,

> God, who knows the heart, bore witness to them, by giving them the Holy Spirit just as he did to us, and he made no distinction between us and them, having cleansed their hearts by faith (vv. 8–9).

Barnabas and Paul also spoke to those gathered and told them how God had done signs and wonders among the Gentiles. Finally, after much deliberation. James spoke to the group, and quoting from a passage in Amos 9, he gave a word of wisdom and told the council what should be done. He directed a letter be written, communicating that the new

Gentile converts should not be troubled but encouraged only "to abstain from the things polluted by idols, and from sexual immorality, and from what has been strangled, and from blood" (v. 20).

THE WORD OF KNOWLEDGE

The second revelatory gift is the **word of knowledge** (or utterance of knowledge). This manifestation is a report or impartation of a specific piece of information that a person could not possibly know by natural means. The word of knowledge will happen in tandem with evangelism, healings, or miracles.

A New Testament example of the word of knowledge happened when Jesus encountered the woman at the well in John 4. This woman was a Samaritan, yet Jesus engaged in a conversation with her. He told her, "Go, call your husband, and come here" (v. 16). The woman replied that she did not have a husband. It was then that Jesus delivered a word of knowledge: "You are right in saying, 'I have no husband'; for you have had five husbands, and the one you now have is not your husband" (vv. 17–18).

DISCERNING OF SPIRITS

The third revelatory gift is the **discerning of spirits** (or gift of discernment). It is the ability to perceive quickly whether such things as people, events, or beliefs are from God or are of demonic origin. In a given environment, through this manifestation, you will be able to tell the kind of spirit that is at work.

While Paul and Silas were ministering in Philippi, a slave girl confronted them with a spirit of divination (see Acts 16:16–18). The two men were carrying out their ministry during the course of a day when this girl starting followed them. She cried out, "These men are servants of the Most High God, who proclaim to you the way of salvation'" (v. 17). She kept up this activity for many days, and Paul became annoyed. He realized through discernment that even though the spirit was speaking truth, it was disrupting their ministry. One day Paul turned around and called out to the spirit, "I command you in the name of Jesus Christ to come out of her" (v. 18). Immediately, the spirit of divination came out of the girl.

Before proceeding into the next cluster of manifestations, I want to show how important these revelatory gifts are in effecting change in our world. We enter and leave many kinds of situations in which we can discern spirits are in operation. We may have words of wisdom or words of knowledge people need in those environments. Oftentimes, however, we walk blindly into places because we are more comfortable operating in our flesh than we are in the power of the Holy Spirit. When that happens by default, whatever spirit is governing that environment begins to influence us. This does not have to happen. If we enter each environment discerning the spirits or listening to the Holy Spirit for words of wisdom and knowledge, then we can activate the Kingdom wherever we go. Then, under the Holy Spirit, we can take authority over the principality or ruler of darkness that has set up shop in that place.

If we enter each environment discerning the spirits or listening to the Holy Spirit for words of wisdom and knowledge, then we can activate the Kingdom wherever we go.

POWER GIFTS

The **power gifts** (or dynamic gifts) are those *charismata* in which God, through the anointing of the Holy Spirit, releases a surge of power (or *dunamis)* into a situation. He does this to address the situation or condition when it is contrary to His will. These gifts may also be called *power manifestations* because of the surge or release of supernatural power to accomplish something God wants to reverse.

THE GIFT OF FAITH

The **gift of faith** is the first power gift. Through it, the Holy Spirit imparts divine faith and confidence in God's will for a specific need or situation, and it often accompanies a gift of "revelation." For example, the blind female pastor from Cuba I wrote about earlier had the gift of faith. It is an infusion of radical trust, which thrusts someone into faith-filled action.

I want you to understand that there are different kinds of faith:

- *Saving faith* or faith for salvation brings about regeneration or rebirth.

- *The fruit of faith* is one of the components of the fruit of the Spirit Paul lists in Galatians 5. He also wrote in his letter to the Romans that faith comes to us as we hear the Word of God, so faith can grow and develop in us as part of the fruit of the Spirit (see Romans 10:17).
- *Miraculous faith* is what Paul wrote about in 1 Corinthians 12. The woman with the issue of blood had this kind of faith—she believed she would be healed if only she could reach Jesus (see Luke 8:43–48). According to Jewish ceremonial law, she was unclean and not supposed to touch anyone, nor was anyone supposed to touch her. She maneuvered her way through the crowd and reached out to touch the hem or the fringe of Jesus' robe. This fringe was known as the *tzitzit*, or one of the robe's corner tassels. The prophet Malachi said, "The sun of righteousness shall rise with healing in its wings" (Malachi 4:2). The Hebrew word translated as 'wings' can also be translated 'tassels on the corners of a garment.' So, by faith, this woman believed that when the Messiah or "the sun of righteousness" came, He would have healing in the fringes of His garment. She pressed through the crowd and touched the *tzitzit*. Then the *dunamis* or power went forth from Jesus and into her body. Though He did not see the woman right away, Jesus said, "Someone touched me, for I perceive that power has gone out from me" (Luke 8:46). Her faith put a demand on His miracle-working power. In response, Jesus said, "Daughter, your faith has made you well; go in peace" (Luke 8:48).

GIFTS OF HEALINGS

The second power gift is the **gifts of healings**. These gifts are the reversal of physical, emotional, and spiritual illnesses.

Bringing about perfect health, they include a variety of impartations through prayer and the laying on of hands. The Greek phrase Paul uses in 1 Corinthians 12 indicates that there are plural gifts or manifestations rather than a singular gift of healing.

Luke wrote, "The people also gathered from the towns around Jerusalem, bringing the sick and those afflicted with unclean spirits, and they were all healed" (Acts 5:16). God healed different people from many towns who were afflicted with various "unclean spirits." That's why I say these are plural *gifts of healings*. God healed a variety of people with many different illnesses, which means He healed them in a variety of ways.

THE WORKING OF MIRACLES

The **working of miracles** is the third power gift. With this gift, God provides the ability to demonstrate the supernatural power of the Holy Spirit and confirm the superiority of the reign of the Kingdom of God over spiritual darkness and even natural law. The best way I know to explain the word *miracles* is that it's *boom!* There is no Greek equivalent for the English word *miracles*. In fact, the most direct translation of the Greek text is literally translated as the *working(s) of power* (*dunamis*). For example, Jesus came into His hometown of Nazareth, and people were astonished. They asked, "Where did this man get this wisdom and these mighty works?" (Matthew 13:54). The mighty works are the same as the working of miracles or signs and wonders.

The New Testament gives four classifications of miracles. The writer of Hebrews says, "God also bore witness by signs and wonders and various miracles and by gifts of the Holy Spirit distributed according to his will" (Hebrews 2:4). Accordingly, these four classifications of miracles include:

- *Signs* (turning water into wine)
- *Wonders* (resurrections from the dead)
- *Miracles* (anything that suspends nature)
- *Gifts* of the Holy Spirit, as all the gifts are miraculous.

All the gifts are miraculous.

Apostolic efforts were often accompanied by the working of miracles, which served to confirm the message of the gospel. The apostle Peter referenced this connection in his sermon on the day of Pentecost:

Men of Israel, hear these words: Jesus of Nazareth, a man attested to you by God with mighty works and wonders and signs that God did through him in your midst, as you yourselves know (Acts 2:22).

The working of miracles can also confirm the apostolic ministry of the gospel. Paul said it most succinctly when he wrote, "The signs of a true apostle were performed among you with utmost patience, with signs and wonders and mighty works" (2 Corinthians 12:12).

VOCAL GIFTS

The **vocal gifts** are gifts of utterance or speech. They are, therefore, speaking gifts, and their purpose is to deliver a message to someone from God. These gifts are not based on human wisdom or understanding. They are supernatural utterances.

THE GIFT OF TONGUES

The **gift of tongues** is a vocal gift or a spiritual utterance given by the Holy Spirit to communicate in a language not previously known or understood by the speaker. The purpose of tongues is to give a message to other believers in order to build them up or strengthen them on behalf of God the Father. There is a difference between the corporate use of the gift of tongues and the use of a spiritual language in personal prayer. As individuals, we pray in the Spirit or in tongues for personal edification. I covered this earlier at the end of School of the Spirit 201. The apostle Paul makes a distinction between personal prayer and tongues spoken in a corporate worship service: "Therefore, one who speaks in a tongue should pray that he may interpret" (1 Corinthians 14:13). Paul was saying that when we are gathered together in a corporate setting, the purpose of speaking in tongues is to deliver a message to build up the whole corporate body. In addition, that message will need an interpretation in order for it to be understood.

> If any speak in a tongue, let there be only two or at most three, and each in turn, and let someone interpret. But if there is no

one to interpret, let each of them keep silent in church and speak to himself and to God (1 Corinthians 14:27–28).

THE GIFT OF INTERPRETATION OF TONGUES

The Holy Spirit has a corresponding gift to the gift of tongues: the **gift of interpretation of tongues.** This gift is the ability to understand and then speak forth the meaning of words previously spoken in an unknown language so that others present may be edified. This gift, then, works in tandem with the gift of tongues. Now, there are times when an individual speaks in tongues and doesn't need an interpreter, because those present corporately understand the words. In other words, the "tongue speaker" doesn't know the language, but under the unction of the Holy Spirit, the individual delivers a word in the tongue (or language) of the hearers.

When the apostle Paul instructed the Corinthian believers, however, about the flow of the gifts in a worship service, he wanted them to do things "decently and in order" (1 Corinthians 14:40). Confusion would abound if individuals often interrupted the worship service with a tongue and no interpretation. People would not know what was happening. Paul seemed to be making a concession for the gift of tongues by acknowledging that God wants others to understand and benefit from it. In order for others to benefit, though, they would have to receive an interpretation of what was said in tongues. While Paul put constraints upon the public gift of tongues for practical reasons, he also said the Church should not forbid it: "So, my brothers, earnestly desire to prophesy, and do not forbid speaking in tongues" (1 Corinthians 14:39).

In my personal experience, when the gift of tongues is used in a corporate setting, it is usually not really a prophetic message to the people, though it can be, as much as it actually is a praise to God. Whenever an individual breaks out in tongues in such a way as to interrupt the service, there should be an interpretation so those gathered can be built up and edified. At Radiant Church, we have had a handful of experiences when a person came to the front of the auditorium and was given the opportunity to speak in tongues and give an interpretation. These have been powerful moments. Even so, we have not routinely encouraged that activity as much as we have urged individuals to prophesy, because that is what Paul did.

THE GIFT OF PROPHECY

This brings us to the last vocal gift—the **gift of prophecy**. Prophecy is the ability to speak forth under the influence of the Holy Spirit a message that brings edification, exhortation, and comfort from the heart of the Father to others. Prophecy is a "now" word from the Holy Spirit, yet it is subject to witness of Scripture. If someone attempts to give a prophetic word that goes against the plain truth of the Bible, then it is not a true prophetic word. Those who do this are either prophesying out of their own soul or being used by the enemy.

As I discussed earlier, the prophet Joel declared that sons and daughters would prophesy in the last days when the Holy Spirit was poured out (see Joel 2:28–29). When we prophesy, it is a fulfillment of Joel's prophecy. It only makes sense, then, that Paul encouraged believers in his day to "earnestly desire the spiritual gifts, especially that you may prophesy" (1 Corinthians 14:1). Prophecy edifies, builds up, encourages, and comforts the hearer. Paul also wrote, "For you can all prophesy one by one, that all may learn and all be encouraged" (1 Corinthians 14:31 NKJV). Prophecy is to the corporate body what personal prayer language is to the individual—it's meant to edify and build up.

> *Prophecy is to the corporate body what personal prayer language is to the individual—it's meant to edify and build up.*

For clarity, I will add that individuals who prophesy aren't necessarily prophets. This is an important distinction. While Paul talked about every believer pursuing the gift of prophecy and all being able to prophesy, there are those individuals who are set apart for prophetic ministry. In Acts, the Holy Spirit separated Barnabas and Saul unto God "for the work to which I have called them" (see Acts 13:2). Those who are prophets have been separated for the work to which they've been called.

//////

Now that we have looked at the three different clusters of gifts, I have something very important to tell you: God wants to use you. He's given you His Holy Spirit, who has gifts available for you. As you walk in step with the Holy Spirit, you will be amazed at the ways, times, places, situations, and people to whom He chooses to use you to impart His gifts as He wills. As Paul said, I encourage you to pursue these gifts for the glory of God and the advancement of His Kingdom on the earth.

Father, You've told us to pursue the gifts we read about in Scripture. Today, we recognize we have done nothing to earn these manifestations of Your Holy Spirit. These are all Your works of grace. Release the gifts of wisdom, knowledge, discernment, faith, healings, miracles, tongues, interpretations of tongues, and prophecy in us for the good of all. May the name of Jesus be exalted in the earth. In Jesus' name, Amen.

STUDY GUIDE

THE WORD FOR GIFTS in the Greek is *charisma(ta)*. It is also the same root word translated as *grace*. Spiritual gifts are supernatural manifestations of God's grace. The Holy Spirit manifests in your gifts and leads you toward your purpose. The nine spiritual gifts in 1 Corinthians 12 can be divided into three types, though these categories are not precise, and gifts in reality often overlap. God may impart one or more of these gifts to you as He wills.

REVIEW

1. Why do you think that spiritual gifts do not seem to be as important to the Church today as they were to the founders of the first century Church?
2. How do spiritual gifts manifest in believers? Which spiritual gifts are available to which believers?
3. What one critical element is necessary to fulfill your purpose or destiny in Christ?

REFLECTION

1. How do you respond to the knowledge that God has shown immense grace to His people by allowing the Holy Spirit to manifest as spiritual gifts?

2. With which type of gifts or specific gift(s) do you feel most connected or comfortable? Why?
3. How will you respond to all you have learned about the Holy Spirit, baptism in the Spirit, and the gifts of the Spirit?

THE SPIRIT-EMPOWERED LIFE

But as it is written:

> *"Eye has not seen, nor ear heard,*
> *Nor have entered into the heart of man*
> *The things which God has prepared for those who love Him."*

But God has revealed them to us through His Spirit. For the Spirit searches all things, yes, the deep things of God. For what man knows the things of a man except the spirit of the man which is in him? Even so no one knows the things of God except the Spirit of God. Now we have received, not the spirit of the world, but the Spirit who is from God, that we might know the things that have been freely given to us by God.

—The apostle Paul in 1 Corinthians 2:9–12 NKJV

AT THE BEGINNING OF THIS BOOK, I told you about the time my grandfather and I went boondoggling in his red Chevy truck. He took me to Richardson's Dairy, and I picked out a Slo Poke Caramel Pop "that was big enough to row a kayak." What I'd really like for you to remember from that story, though, is the question I asked him before he bought it for me: "Grandpa, what *do* I want?"

Now you know all that is available for you through the Holy Spirit, including the baptism, the gifts, the direction, the power, the guidance, the help, the signs, and the miracles. I think it would be fitting to turn to your heavenly Father and ask Him a little different version of that question: "Father, what do *You* want?"

The examples I have given from the Scripture of those who lived asking that question means that the Father also has a great adventure planned for you. He wants you to live the Spirit-empowered life, which means you will be living beyond yourself. In living a life beyond yourself you will have a life of faith, trust, and dependence upon the Holy Spirit that overflows with the supernatural. When you live a life beyond yourself, it also produces an outcome that causes the people looking at you to say, "God must have done this." There is no other explanation for who you are, where you are, or what you've done. That is the best witness you can give to the world.

Jesus came in part to establish a pattern for our lives. He wants us to live in full cooperation with the Father through the Holy Spirit. We will be living lives beyond ourselves—lives of faith with no natural explanation for what is happening. The only explanation we can give is there must be something supernatural going on.

Our world conditions us not to live lives beyond ourselves, but rather beyond our means, which always results in debt. We're constantly told the thing that will satisfy us, give us significance, or fill our souls will come to us if we grab ahold of those things that will help us gain the approval of others. We think we will get elevated to some position or place of wealth, power, fame, or acceptance. The apostle John wrote,

> Do not love the world or the things in the world. If anyone loves the world, the love of the Father is not in him. For all that *is*

in the world—the lust of the flesh, the lust of the eyes, and the pride of life—is not of the Father but is of the world. And the world is passing away, and the lust of it; but he who does the will of God abides forever (1 John 2:15–17 NKJV).

When we live a life beyond our means, we end up giving our energies and our passions toward the things of the flesh. We allow the direction of our lives to be shaped and motivated by the things we think will satisfy us, things that are temporal in nature. But none of these produce an overflow; rather, they produce a deficiency.

When you live a life beyond your means, you live in debt spiritually, emotionally, and physically. But when you live a life beyond yourself, you will produce an overflow of the fruit of the Spirit: "love, joy, peace, longsuffering, kindness, goodness, faithfulness, gentleness, [and] self-control" (Galatians 5:22–23 NKJV). You will live a Spirit-empowered life that has a supernatural explanation, not a life that needs a supernatural bailout.

> *You will live a Spirit-empowered life that has a supernatural explanation, not a life that needs a supernatural bailout.*

Jesus is our pattern. He lived a life of perfect obedience, but not obedience to a system. His obedience was to the Father through the empowerment of the Holy Spirit, and that is a drastically different way to live. Religion tells us to obey a system with outward actions, but the motivation is really fear.

Faith, on the other hand, starts on the inside and works its way out. Faith has an overflow.

Religion says there's nothing else for you to do but be a good Christian, read your Bible, avoid sin, and go to church. That's the problem, though—there *is* nothing else for you to do. And that can leave a sense of dissatisfaction inside you saying, "But I wanted to live an adventure." One of the devil's major schemes against your life once you're saved is to get you ensnared in religion and bored by it. That's when the things of the world start to have a pull on you.

God doesn't want a religious life for you. Religious traditions will keep you from the great adventure. I urge you to continue on in the School of the Spirit. You won't become bored. With the power of the Holy Spirit upon you, you now have a destiny and calling. You are called to live the Spirit-empowered life with the outflow of the overflow and with the manifestation of the gifts. It will be a life beyond yourself because you walk in step with the Holy Spirit, and He directs you. He advises you, guides you, and endues you with power from on high. He will even arrange divine appointments and hand out divine assignments. Your response is to partner with Him to fulfill the Great Commission until Jesus comes.

Father, thank You for calling us to live beyond ourselves. Help us be carriers of the presence and power of the Holy Spirit. Teach us to be salt and light for Your Kingdom. Make us shine brightly and be radiant, carrying Your glory into the darkness of the world and dispelling the works of the enemy. May Your Kingdom come and Your will be done in our lives and on the earth. For Yours is the Kingdom, the power, and the glory forever. In Jesus' name, Amen.

10 FREQUENTLY ASKED QUESTIONS

WHENEVER I CONDUCT a School of the Spirit at Radiant Church, I solicit questions from the participants on topics related to the Holy Spirit and the baptism in the Holy Spirit. I've included 10 of the most frequently asked questions and their corresponding answers below. My hope is that these will give you even more understanding.

1. **What is the difference between speaking in tongues, the baptism in the Holy Spirit, and the promise of the Father?**

   The promise of the Father is identical to *the baptism in the Holy Spirit*. Both of these refer to the Holy Spirit's coming upon individuals and enduing them "with power from on high" (see Luke 24:49). The book of Acts shows a pattern of the Holy Spirit coming upon people subsequent to salvation. It doesn't replace salvation; rather, it is something additional. Speaking in tongues is a gift of the Holy Spirit. Again, in the book of Acts, when people were baptized in the Holy Spirit, there was a corresponding outflow of the overflow. This outflow was a spiritual utterance referred to as *speaking in tongues*. I also told you about how the term *praying in the Spirit* refers to speaking in tongues. We need to see tongues or spiritual utterance not so much as a proof of the baptism in the Holy Spirit but rather as a privilege and a promise to every believer.

2. **Do you have to have received water baptism before receiving the baptism in the Holy Spirit?**

No, the Bible gives an example of people who received the baptism in the Holy Spirit before they were water baptized. In Acts 10, we read about Peter going to the home of Cornelius the centurion. Somewhere in the middle of Peter's sermon, the audience was convicted by his words. The Holy Spirit fell on them, and they all began to speak in tongues and prophesy. Afterward, Peter baptized them in water.

Typically, someone is saved, baptized in water, and then baptized in the Holy Spirit. So the occurrence at the home of Cornelius was outside the norm. However, this example demonstrates to us that a person may be saved and then baptized in the Spirit before being water baptized. In any case, Spirit baptism is subsequent to salvation.

3. **I feel like a doubter about tongues. I'm waiting for the gift, yet I'm trying to believe it will come. Am I just not ready?**

The first thing I say to someone who asks this question is, "Give yourself a break." You're a child of God, and this is part of your inheritance. There's nothing wrong with you. You may have some doubts but remember that one of the things that will help you receive the gift of tongues is to be convinced. How can you be convinced? First, don't accept doubt. Dig into the Word of God, because it will build your faith. The Bible will tell you what belongs to you and what is available to you. It will remind you of God's faithfulness and character.

Right now, the greatest manifestation of the Holy Spirit you may experience is the peace of God as you study His Word. The Holy Spirit will convince your heart of its truth. Remember, part of His job is to lead and guide you into all truth (see John 16:13). Don't give into pressure, whether it comes from you or someone else.

As you study the Scriptures with sincerity and allow the Holy Spirit to teach you, God will help you. Then you will be able to open up your heart. Speaking in tongues will be easy because, technically, you already have this gift at your disposal. It's been made available to you, and it is part of your inheritance. Sometimes, according to God's purposes, speaking in tongues simply takes some people a little more time than others. For example, it's not uncommon for those who are intellectually and logically minded to need more convincing, more studying, and more understanding before they are convinced and open to receiving this gift.

4. **How should I refer to speaking in tongues?**

If you've ever had a conversation with somebody who doesn't have the gift of speaking in tongues, you know firsthand how difficult it can be to talk about it. I recognize that it is controversial to many people. When you bring up the word *tongues*, some people will act as if you're talking about something very strange. I would encourage you to use the phrases *spiritual utterance* or *spiritual language* instead. This approach is not intended to encourage dishonesty or to insinuate there's anything for which you should be embarrassed or ashamed. We are not ashamed of the gospel, nor are we ashamed of the baptism in the Holy Spirit. We are not embarrassed by any of His gifts. Nevertheless, I recommend changing the terminology because *tongues* is an old English word that we don't use conversationally in the same way the original usage was intended. For example, we don't ask someone, "What tongue do you speak?" Instead, we ask, "What language do you speak?" However, 400 years ago, when the King James Version of the Bible was translated, people would have talked about the tongue someone spoke, and they would have meant language.

Sadly in today's culture, the terminology of speaking in tongues is usually used as a religious phrase with much associated baggage. For some people, the word will not be an obstacle. For others, however, the term could be an unnecessary impediment to the conversation about this wonderful gift. When you change the phraseology, suddenly, you will not find an immediate barrier. So I encourage you to speak about spiritual language or spiritual utterance.

5. **How do I know when it's really God telling me to witness to someone?**

If it pops into your mind and you feel an urge to witness, then you should witness or share your faith. Our minds are not predisposed toward things of the Spirit. I have found that if I'm thinking about helping someone or talking to someone about God, then I should act on those thoughts. First, I immediately begin to pray about what the Spirit is telling me, asking Him for wisdom and discernment about how to approach the person. In other words, I prepare my heart. Then I follow His lead. Often, I begin the conversation with the individual He's directed my attention toward. Always remember that kindness goes a long way when you are sharing your faith or when you help someone.

6. **When laying hands on someone to receive the baptism in the Holy Spirit, do you have to pray in the Spirit in order for them to receive it?**

Though we read of the instances when the apostles laid hands on believers and they received the Holy Spirit, we also read that God baptized others in the Spirit without anyone laying hands on them or anyone praying in the Spirit over or with them. So, no, you don't have to pray in the Spirit for someone to receive the baptism.

Again, walking in step with the Spirit is important. Before you pray for someone, ask God, "How do You want me to do this?" It may be that He wants you to place your hand on an individual's shoulder and then they will receive. I have found that praying in the Spirit can be helpful as you are praying for someone to receive the gift of tongues. First, it helps you to allow the Holy Spirit to pray the will of the Father through you. It can also be a means to intercede for the individual. However, I've also found it provides sound that can take some of the pressure off the person for whom you are praying. Quietness can create pressure and a feeling of awkwardness. Praying in the Spirit helps the individual receiving prayer and relieves the pressure, allowing them to join right in when they begin to speak in tongues. Simply be sensitive to the Holy Spirit and follow His lead.

7. **If I'm praying, when should I pray to the Father, to Jesus, and to the Holy Spirit?**

Jesus taught us to pray to the Father in Jesus' name (see Matthew 6:9; Luke 11:2). I would say that when you pray and petition God for something, you should pray to the Father in Jesus' name. However, you can call on the name of Jesus like some did in the Gospels. Blind Bartimaeus, for example, cried out, "Jesus, Son of David, have mercy on me!" (Mark 10:47). And, by the way, it resulted in his being healed. Also, it's totally appropriate to worship all three members of the Trinity—Father, Son, and Holy Spirit. Oftentimes, when I'm praying devotionally, I recognize and welcome the Holy Spirit.

8. **Do we really have access to all the gifts of the Spirit Paul lists in 1 Corinthians 12?**

   The short answer is yes! Paul wrote, "All these are empowered by one and the same Spirit, who apportions to each one individually as he wills" (1 Corinthians 12:11). These gifts are manifestations of the Holy Spirit, and if you have the Holy Spirit, then you have all these manifestations available to you, subject to the will of the Holy Spirit in any given situation. I want to emphasize the last part of this statement: the gifts are available to you because the Holy Spirit indwells you, but their being used or exercised by you are subject to the will of the Holy Spirit. He is the administrator of the gifts.

9. **Do you have any practical advice for the use of discernment and wisdom in a professional work setting?**

   Obviously, you should do your job well. God has called you to be submitted to authority and stay within the boundaries of your job description. But you will want to look for ways to invade your work environment with the Holy Spirit. For example, you can walk into an office and pray in the Spirit under your breath. You can even make declarations in a very quiet voice, stating that the will of God be done there as it is in heaven. Even before you go to work, pray in the Spirit and with understanding for your day, your co-workers, and your employer or company. Go into your workday having asked and believed for wisdom and discernment. Ask the Holy Spirit to lead you and to help you see open doors to share His love or encourage others in your workplace. Go in with your heart and ears open to your environment and to the Holy Spirit. Showing kindness and compassion to those around you is letting your light shine. If you go in with a heart to serve the Father, the Holy Spirit will navigate you through what you say or do and to whom you say it or do it. Pay attention to His nudges and listen to the inner witness of His voice.

10. **What causes people to have unusual manifestations in some church meetings? Are these manifestations of the Spirit?**

Yes, they can be. Throughout the history of the Church, during awakenings or revivals, there were unique or extraordinary manifestations. For example, in Acts 2, there were flames of fire appearing upon the heads of those gathered when the Holy Spirit was poured out. As we read from some of the journals or historical accounts of the two Great Awakenings in America and of the later revivals like Azusa Street or the Latter Rain, we find some people would tremble or shake under the convicting power of the Holy Spirit. Some people would fall down or seem to have fainted while encountering the presence of God. Still others would yell because the intense conviction of sin came upon them. Remember, John on the island of Patmos fell down as though he were dead when he encountered the glorified form of Jesus (see Revelation 1:17).

The manifest presence of God on a person can affect them, causing them to shake, tremble, rock, or fall down. If we try to measure spiritual encounters by the lens of our natural minds, we will find ways to disprove them every time. But if we understand that the presence of God affects our physical bodies in different ways, then we can embrace what happens to others during times of revival, outpourings of the Spirit, or other God-encounters. Therefore, it's important to grow in your sensitivity to the Holy Spirit and ask Him for discernment so that you can know when something is a result of someone encountering God or something else.

ENDNOTES

MAKING THE CONNECTION

1. Encyclopaedia Britannica Online, s.v. "Nicene Creed," Updated May 15, 2020, https://www.britannica.com/topic/Nicene-Creed. The First Council of Nicaea (AD 325 developed a basic and ecumenical statement of faith, which means it has been widely used by Christians around the world.

2. Mary Fairchild, "How Many Christians Are In the World Today?," Learn Religions, April 16, 2020, https://www.learnreligions .com/christianity-statistics-700533.

3. Todd M. Johnson and Gina A. Zurlo, eds. World Christian Database (Leiden/Boston: Brill, accessed July 2018), http://www .worldchristiandatabase.org.

4. Mary Fairchild, "How Many Christians Are In the World Today?"

5. Mark Ellis, "'Fastest-Growing Church' Has No Buildings, No Central Leadership, and Is Mostly Led by Women," The Christian Post, September 23, 2019, https://www.christianpost.com/news /fastest-growing-church-has-no-buildings-no-central-leadership -and-is-mostly-led-by-women.html.

6. "Muslims Turning to Christ Across the Middle East," CBN News, January 12, 2017, https://www1.cbn.com/cbnnews/cwn/2017 /january/muslims-turning-to-christ-across-the-middle-east.

7. Philosophers and social scientists refer to this western phenomenon as the "disenchantment of the world." The modernist philosophy birthed out of the Enlightenment and the elevation of the scientific and empirical methods have prejudiced society against the claims of religion, spirituality, and the supernatural. The Enlightenment juxtaposed science and religion and made the claims of the two mutually exclusive. This belief is so common that most western Christians have even adopted some form of it. Many Christian scholars and scientists have tried to bridge this gap, but this mode of thinking still exists in the minds of many people in the Western world.

8. The empirical method and the scientific method are sometimes confused with each other. They are the same minus one exception. The empirical method is broader in scope. Whereas the scientific method is based on experiments using physically measurable objects and tests, the empirical method looks at evidence based on a collection of data.

9. Indulgences were a way for people to pay the Catholic Church to forgive sins and restore themselves to God. Not only did Luther oppose this practice on the grounds that it was unbiblical, but it also discouraged people from giving to the poor instead.

10. One term used for translating into the languages of the people was the "vernacular," which means the ordinary language of a people in a particular region. This desire to translate the Bible continues today through the work of many Bible agencies and Christian translation organizations. If people need to understand the Bible, the best way is for them to be able to read and study it in their own languages.

11. Tony Lane, "A Man for All People: Introducing William Tyndale: Christian History Magazine" (Christian History Institute), accessed November 20, 2020, https://christianhistoryinstitute.org /magazine/article/a-man-for-all-people.

YOUR ADVANTAGE

1. John Foxe, *Foxe's Christian Martyrs of the World; the Story of the Advance of Christianity from Bible Times to Latest Periods of Persecution.* (Philadelphia: C. Foster Publishing Co, 1907).

YOUR PARTNER

1. "Richland, Michigan Population: Census 2010 and 2000 Interactive Map, Demographics, Statistics, Quick Facts," Census Viewer, accessed December 9, 2020, http://censusviewer.com/city /MI/Richland.

THE PROMISE OF THE FATHER

1. "Synoptic" means to see with the same eye. Matthew, Mark, and Luke share many of the same stories and generally follow the same sequence. The Gospel of John tells many stories and relates many events that do not occur in the other Gospels. While they are not contradictory accounts, they are different in nature and substance.

THE OUTPOURING OF THE HOLY SPIRIT

1. "Ketubah Text," Sefaria, accessed December 16, 2020, https://www.sefaria.org/Ketubah_Text?lang=bi.
2. Moshe Weissman, *The Midrash Says: Shemot.* (Brooklyn: Bnay Yakov Publications, 1995), 182.

3. "Shemot Rabbah 5:9," Sefaria, accessed December 15, 2020, https://www.sefaria.org/Shemot_Rabbah.5.9?lang=bi. See also Dustin Herron, "Tongues of Fire and 70 Languages," May 26, 2017, https://firm.org.il/learn/tongues-fire-70-languages.

SCRIPTURE INDEX

2:39, *5*
3:4, *155*
3:6, *155*
4:31, *125*
5:12, *91*
5:14, *91*
5:15–16, *155*
5:16, *175*
7, *115*
7:58, *115*
8, *108*
8:1, *115*
8:3, *115*
8:14–17, *108*
8:19, *109*
8:24, *110*
9, *115*
9:1–2, *115*
9:4–6, *115*
9:15, *116*
9:17, *116*
10, *110, 190*
10:4–6, *110*
10:11–13, *110*
10:15, *111*
10:19–20, *111*
10:23, *111*
10:38, *xxii*
10:44–46, *111*
13:2, *180*
15, *170*
15:8–9, *170*
16:16–18, *172*
16:17, *172*
16:18, *172*
19, *112*
19:2, *112, 128*
19:3, *113*
19:4–6, *113*

Romans
8:7, *132*
8:14, *57*

8:26–27, *60*
8:28, *43*
10:17, *174*
11, *105*

1 Corinthians
2:9–12, *185*
2:12, *56*
6:3, *47*
6:11, *29*
6:19, *21*
12, *62, 165, 174-175, 183, 194*
12:3, *23*
12:3–11, *166*
12:4–6, *62*
12:4–7, *64*
14:1, *130, 180*
14:2, *132*
14:4, *130*
12:11, *194*
14:12, *163*
14:13, *177*
14:14, *132*
14:15, *132*
14:27–28, *178*
14:31, *180*
14:39, *178*
14:40, *178*

2 Corinthians
3:17, *38*
4:5–7, *51*
5:17, *38*
10:5, *65*
12:12, *176*

Galatians
5, *161, 174*
6, *153*
6:8, *130*
5:16–18, *150*
5:22–23, *165, 187*
5:25, *150*

ABOUT THE AUTHOR

LEE M. CUMMINGS is the founding and senior pastor of Radiant Church, a multisite church reaching the globe via Radiant Church campuses and online at www.radiant.church.

In addition to his role at Radiant, Lee serves as an overseer and mentor to many next-generation leaders and church planters. It was this role that led to the launch of the Radiant Network, of which Lee is founder and president. Since that launch in June of 2016, churches across the United States and North America call themselves Radiant Church, and many more have joined the Radiant Network family of churches.

Lee and his wife, Jane, started Radiant Church in 1996, in a high school gymnasium in Richland, Michigan (a rural community on the outskirts of Kalamazoo). Since then, Radiant Church has grown to reach thousands of people in several locations, all with the same mission: to lead people to become radiant disciples of Jesus Christ.

As a highly respected leader in the Church, Lee speaks frequently at leadership events, conferences, and churches worldwide. He is the author of the highly acclaimed books *Be Radiant, Flourish: Planting Your Life Where God Designed it to Grow,* and *School of the Spirit: Living the Holy Spirit-Empowered Life.*

Lee and Jane were married in 1992 and have three grown children, two sons-in-law, and one grandson. They reside in Kalamazoo, Michigan.

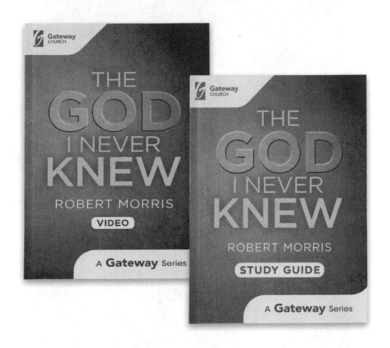

MORE FROM LEE M. CUMMINGS

Be Radiant is a prophetic call for the church to arise and shine as the light of the world, and become a Radiant City on a hill. As Christians, every one of us has a unique and important role to play in bringing God's glory to a world that is groping in darkness. Discover how to engage your culture with the power and love of God— adding light and color to the darkness.

Available wherever books are sold.

MORE FROM LEE M. CUMMINGS

God has designed everything in created order to thrive in the right environment. Fish were made for the sea, birds for the air, and we were made to thrive in the presence of God. *Flourish* explores and unpacks how God has designed us to thrive when we are planted deep in the root system of the local church, and therein living Spirit-filled, Spirit-led lives of abundance and nearness to the Father's heart.

Available wherever books are sold.